B　　　　Haskins, James　　　T3598
You

　　　Andrew Young; a man with a
　mission

Andrew Young
Man with a Mission

LOTHROP BOOKS BY JAMES HASKINS

Andrew Young: *Man with a Mission*

The Life and Death of Martin Luther King, Jr.

The Story of Stevie Wonder
   (*winner of the Coretta Scott King award*)

Jobs in Business and Office

From Lew Alcindor to Kareem Abdul-Jabbar

Babe Ruth and Hank Aaron: *The Home Run Kings*

Bob McAdoo, Superstar

Andrew Young
Man with a Mission

James Haskins

Lothrop, Lee & Shepard Company
A Division of William Morrow & Co., Inc. New York

Library of Congress Cataloging in Publication Data

Haskins, James, (date)
  Andrew Young, man with a mission.

  Includes index.
  SUMMARY: An account of the life of Andrew Young, including his activities
as a clergyman, civil rights worker, legislator, and United States Ambassador
to the United Nations.
  1. Young, Andrew J., 1932-   —Juvenile literature. 2. Ambassadors—United
States—Biography—Juvenile literature. 3. Legislators—United States—Biography
—Juvenile literature. 4. United States. Congress. House—House—Biography—
Juvenile literature. 5. United Church of Christ—Clergy—Biography—Juvenile
literature. [1. Young, Andrew J., 1932-   . 2. Statesmen. 3. Afro-Americans—
Biography] I. Title.
E840.8.Y64H37   973.92092'4 [B] [92]   79-1046
ISBN 0-688-41896-1   ISBN 0-688-51896-6 lib. bdg.

ACKNOWLEDGMENTS

Grateful acknowledgment is made for permission to reprint materials as follows:

Excerpts from "We Will Return" by Andrew Levison (January 8, 1973); "Up the Short Ladder" (May 21, 1973); and "Why I Support Jimmy Carter" by Andrew Young (April 3, 1976) © 1973 & 1976 by *The Nation*. Reprinted by permission of *The Nation*.

Excerpts from "A Southern Activist Goes to the House" by Hamilton Bims (February 1973) and "A Close Encounter with Andrew Young" by Herschel Johnson (April 1978) reprinted by permission of *Ebony* Magazine, © 1973 & 1978 by Johnson Publishing Company, Inc.

Excerpts from "Our New Voice at the U.N." by Joseph Lelyveld (February 6, 1977) © 1977 by the New York Times Company. Reprinted by permission.

Excerpts from *My Soul Is Rested* by Howell Raines © 1977 by Howell Raines. Reprinted by permission of G. P. Putnam's Sons.

Excerpts from *The Bonds* by Roger M. Williams © 1972 by Roger M. Williams. Reprinted by permission of Atheneum Publishers.

I am grateful to Mrs. Jean Young, Dr. and Mrs. Andrew Young, Sr., Mrs. Idella Childs, Mrs. Norma de Paur, Bernard Lee, Stoney Cooks and, of course, Andrew Young himself for their time and their help, and to Kathy Benson for her assistance.

Contents

1 / The Walter Winchell
of Cleveland Street

On January 31, 1977, Andrew Jackson Young, Jr., walked up to Secretary-General of the United Nations Kurt Waldheim and presented his credentials as the new United States Ambassador to the United Nations. The act in itself was not particularly noteworthy. There have been many U.S. ambassadors to the U.N., and usually each time a new President moves into the White House he chooses a new ambassador. But President Jimmy Carter had chosen a rather exceptional man. First, he was the only Church of Christ minister to hold the position. Second, he was the first man in the job who had ever been an organizer of a demonstration against U.S. foreign policy, and a demonstration at the U.N. at that. And third, he was the first black ever to hold that post and thus was the highest black official in United States history.

Forty-four years earlier, on March 12, 1932, when Andrew Young was born, the idea that a black man could ever occupy such a high position in the United States was about as far-fetched as the idea that men could ever walk on the moon. Still, Mrs. Andrew Young, Sr., remembers feeling that her first son was rather special. Perhaps it is just hindsight, but she now says, "I always knew Andrew was going to do *something* important."

Andrew Young was luckier than most black children born in the South at that time. His grandfather had been a success-ful businessman in the town of Franklin, Louisiana, operating a drugstore, a pool hall, a saloon, and sponsoring boat trips up the bayous. With the money he made, he was able to send his son to college. Andrew's father, Dr. Andrew Young, Sr., was a dentist, and that meant the Youngs were part of the upper class of New Orleans black society. As Dr. Young ex-plains, "You had to be a professional to live with any kind of dignity in the South, and medicine was the only profession that was really open to blacks. Black lawyers didn't get much business, but there was always a need for doctors and den-tists."

Despite the comparative dignity of their social position, the Youngs suffered many indignities in New Orleans. Blacks were segregated in many ways. When they went downtown, they could not eat in the white restaurants or use the white rest-rooms. They could not go to the white libraries or the white parks. On the city buses, they had to go past the board that divided the seats into "Colored Only" and "Whites Only" sections and sit in the back. And although they lived in a white neighborhood, it was a poor white neighborhood. They would not have been allowed to live in a better white area. Andrew and his brother, Walter, who was born two and a half years later, were the richest children on the block, the only

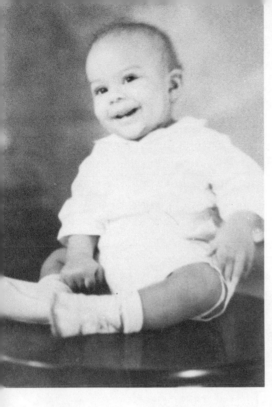

Andrew at nine months. Says his mother: "I always knew Andrew was going to do something important."

(COURTESY OF
DR. AND MRS. ANDREW J. YOUNG)

ones with a basketball hoop and the only ones with spending money.

When Andrew and Walter were very young, they were unaware of racial differences. They played with the Irish and Italian children on Cleveland Street. The white children came to their house and they went to the white children's houses. "But we didn't let them go too far into their houses, especially when we couldn't see what was going on," says Dr. Young. Even well-meaning white neighbors sometimes created problems.

"Once, the mother of one of the children told him, 'Oh, Andrew, your Daddy is so nice—just like a white man,'" Mrs. Young recalls. "So Andrew and I were walking down the street one time—he must have been about four years old—and I saw a young black man we knew. I said, 'Oh, there's Leonard. He's such a nice young man.' And Andrew turned to me and said, 'Mother, is Leonard a white man?' When I got home

I told my husband, 'Our poor child is associating *white* with *nice* because of these people. We've got to move out of this neighborhood!'"

The Youngs did not move, at least not for a long time, but as it turned out their children did not suffer. There was no real racial friction between the Young boys and their white playmates. "I think the reason Andrew gets along so well with white people is that he grew up with them and learned to understand them," says Mrs. Young. "The only racial disturbances on the block occurred when people from outside the neighborhood would come and see those two little black boys playing in a group of white boys. And then they'd yell at them, 'Nigger!' We taught our boys that such people didn't know any better, that they were white people who were insecure about their own race. Andrew wasn't taught to hate."

Andrew, six, and Walter, four. The parents of most of their white playmates could not afford such things as cowboy suits for their children.

(COURTESY OF
DR. AND MRS. ANDREW J. YOUNG)

As small boys Andrew and Walter had both cowboy suits and Indian outfits. Perhaps that kind of early experience taught Andrew to see both sides of most arguments later on.

(COURTESY OF
DR. AND MRS. ANDREW J. YOUNG)

The Youngs were a religious family. Mrs. Young, who was born in New Orleans, had taught Sunday school at Central Congregational Church since the age of fourteen and was superintendent of the Sunday school by the time her children were old enough to go. Dr. Young sang in the choir. Both boys went to Sunday school and later they both sang in the choir. "We always had a rule in our house that if you didn't go to church Sunday morning you didn't go to the movies Sunday afternoon," says Mrs. Young. That rule, coupled with the fact that their mother was superintendent of the Sunday school, effectively assured the boys' excellent attendance records. They were awarded many certificates for perfect attendance.

"But I think the most important religious influence in their lives was my mother," says Mrs. Young. "When the boys were little, she'd sit them down on the front steps and talk to them. She'd always tell them, 'God's gonna take care of you.'"

Dr. and Mrs. Young were not quite so trusting. "I was

given a kind of absolutist morality," recalls Andrew Young. "My parents would tell me, 'You're black, so you can't be half right. You can't even be ninety percent right. You must be two hundred percent right. And even then, any time you argue with a white, you'll be wrong.'"

There were times when his parents wondered if Andrew might not be taking their advice a little too seriously. "He never hesitated to join an adult conversation," says Mrs. Young. "He thought he knew something about everything. We started calling him Walter Winchell [after a renowned newspaper columnist and broadcaster of that time]."

Mrs. Young chuckles, "His brother thought Andrew knew everything, too. Walter would ask me a question, and after I'd answered he'd turn to Andrew and say, 'Is that right?'"

Andrew was a very precocious child, and his parents encouraged him, usually. There was a nursery school nearby, Mrs. Young recalls. "When he was about two and a half years old he decided he wanted to go over there. He loved children and he kept saying, 'I want to go to school! I want to go to school!' So even though he was awfully young, we just let him go over there. We thought he would just play. But because he was so precocious he soon outgrew the nursery school. When he was three years old, they sent him to kindergarten. Hill School was operated by my church, and they had a kindergarten and a first grade. By the time he was four, they had him in first grade, and by the time he was six he was reading comic books to his little brother."

Andrew was in third grade by that time, two or three years younger than most of his classmates, four to six years younger than those who had been left back. It was not always easy being so much younger than the rest, but looking back, Andrew Young feels that the experience was helpful to him. "Adjustment to other people is something I've done all my life," he points out. He formed lasting friendships with a few of his classmates, among them Tom Dent, whom he had met in kindergarten and who would sometimes stay overnight at the Young s so he and Andrew could play together.

Once Andrew learned to read, he read a lot more than comic books. His parents surrounded their boys with books, and Andrew read everything he could find. His father got both boys library cards and took them regularly to the Negro library. His father encouraged Andrew to express himself well, for knowledge is powerful only when it can be expressed. "I never made a public speech in my life," says Dr. Young, "but I wanted him to be able to do so. So I used to stand him on the front steps. He must have been about five when we started. I'd tell him to say, 'Ladies and gentlemen,' and he'd say *'Ladies and gentlemen!'* He was plenty confident."

Andrew, six, and Walter, four. By that time, Andrew was in third grade and was reading comic books to his younger brother.
(COURTESY OF DR. AND MRS. ANDREW J. YOUNG)

Andrew was confident in other ways, too. He loved sports and would try anything he saw the older boys doing. He was, as his father puts it, an "all-around American boy." Dr. Young was on the board of directors of the local black YMCA, which operated a summer camp in Waveland, Mississippi. Andrew began going to that camp at the age of five and he learned to swim his first summer there.

"He never feared anything," says his mother. "He just went right into the water and started swimming. And as he grew older, he played ball with the other boys, and got into fights like a normal boy does."

Because he and Walter always stuck together, the fights were often between the Young boys and the others, and so they were usually outnumbered. "Andrew said he had to learn to protect himself since the odds were one hundred to two," says Dr. Young, "so I set up a boxing ring in the yard and I got the best boxer in the area to teach the boys how to fight. I figured they should know how to fight because of the conditions in the neighborhood."

By hiring the boxer, Dr. Young was putting into practice a saying that was a favorite of his and that he often told his sons. "Don't get mad, get smart," he would say. Andrew came to accept that advice as very practical, but after a while he decided that learning how to box was not the smartest way to protect himself. "I learned that negotiating was better than fighting," he says.

Ordinarily, all the children in the neighborhood got along fine, and it was fun growing up on Cleveland Street. "On Canal Street, one block away from where we lived, there was a cookie factory," Mrs. Young recalls, "and when those cookies began to bake, you could smell the aroma for blocks. Andrew and Walter would come running into the house crying, 'Do you have a nickel?' and they'd take that nickel and all the children would run over to the factory and a lady there would give them a great big bag of broken cookies."

As they grew older, the children became more aware of their racial differences. When it came time to go to school, the white children went to a white school and the Young children went to a black school. When the children were old enough to ride their bikes down to the city park, they learned that the Young boys could not go because blacks were not allowed in the park.

"It was hard for them not to go to the park with the others," Mrs. Young says. "And there were other places. We used to take them riding, and we'd go by places where they wanted to stop. And we'd have to tell them we couldn't stop. So when they were old enough we started taking them to places where they *could* go, so they would have something to tell their friends about. When the summer came, we would take a vacation and let them have new experiences."

Dr. Young recalls, "We took them to New York. We wanted them to be able to experience the things that they were denied at home—like going into the nice restaurants and hotels. I remember when we went into the restaurants they would never bother to read the left side of the menu. They'd just look at the prices on the right. They'd find the most expensive price and say, 'This oughta be good.' And that's what they'd order!"

The Young boys were lucky that their parents could take them to places like New York. Most of the white families in the neighborhood could not afford such trips. Nor could the families of most of their classmates at the black Wilona C. Jones Elementary School.

"Almost all of my classmates were poor, on welfare," Andrew recalls. "I remember when I was in third grade, two of us were sent to the principal for misbehaving. I was six and the other boy was twelve. We had been cutting up in the back of the room, playing mumbledy-peg with a knife. The principal said we had a choice between getting a whipping or going home to get our parents. We both left. My mother gave

Andrew, twelve, and family. Because, as blacks, there were so many things they could not do in the South, the Young boys were taken by their parents to places like New York where they could eat in nice restaurants and sit wherever they wanted to on the buses.

(COURTESY OF DR. AND MRS. ANDREW J. YOUNG)

me a whipping and took me back to school. The other boy never came back. The next time I saw him I was home from college. He had needle tracks on his arms. He had never been back to school since that day in third grade."

When Andrew was fourteen, the Youngs moved. Dr. Young kept his dental office on Cleveland Street, but they now lived in another predominantly white neighborhood on Annette Street, where they live today. It was right near Dillard University, and the boys would ride their bikes over to the campus of the black school and play ball.

Andrew played all sorts of sports and was an excellent swimmer. But he was always so much younger and smaller than his classmates that he never made an athletic team in high school. "The coach would call my daddy every summer to see if I'd gained any weight," he says. But he never got big enough to make a team.

If he didn't gain weight, it was no fault of his. One of the main things his mother remembers about him at that time was that he was always hungry. "I was a great baker," she says. "I'd make rolls regularly, and whenever he would see me making rolls he would get his quart of milk and sit there at the table waiting until the rolls came out of the oven. The minute they came out, he'd start eating."

He was far more interested in eating and in sports than he was in school. "We'd do just enough not to get thrown out," Andrew recalls. His father remembers, "He had the potential, but he just didn't develop it. He used to say he could sit in anybody's class and know what they were going to say before they said it."

One reason Andrew Young knew so much was that he was an avid reader. He did not read just what his teachers told him to. At an age when most schoolchildren are reading about George Washington and Thomas Jefferson, Andrew was reading, on his own, about Ralph Bunche. A black man who had received the first Ph.D. in political science granted to a black American, Bunche had become the first black person to hold a desk job (rather than a janitorial job) with the U.S. Department of State. In 1944 he was an adviser at the meeting of nations that laid the groundwork for the first United Nations session in San Francisco in 1945, and in 1946 he went to work for the United Nations, first on loan from the Department of State and then with a permanent appointment as director of the division that oversaw all the former colonies of U.N. member nations. He would go on to become the first black to win the Nobel Prize for Peace, an international award, for his work in getting Egypt and Israel to sign an armistice, a peace agreement that would last for nearly twenty years.

When Andrew Young was growing up, there were few black heroes. That was partly because black people were denied equal education and employment opportunities and so did not get the chance to become important or famous. It was also partly because black history was not taught in schools and major newspapers and magazines did not pay much attention to current contributions by black people. Even the accomplishments of a man like Dr. Ralph Bunche were under-reported, if indeed they were reported at all, in southern newspapers. But through his own curiosity and independent reading Andrew Young had found a really great man with whom to identify.

Still, his lack of concern with his school subjects worried his parents. His father was particularly worried because he wanted Andrew to be a doctor or a dentist, and he knew his son would have to make good grades in order to get into medical school. His mother was not as singleminded about the matter as her husband, although she, too, wanted her older son to have a successful career. She would not have minded had Andrew leaned toward the ministry, and looking back, she sees now that he had the makings of a minister and had experiences in his early teens that might have directed him to that calling.

"He was always very concerned about the welfare and condition of other human beings," she says. "When he was a little bitty fellow, we had some old people in our church and he would say things like, 'Let's go see Miss Pierce and talk to her. She's so old and lonely.' "

He worked with younger people in the Sunday school and was a member of the youth choir, and because of his grandmother he knew the Bible by heart.

"My mother was blind the last three or four years of her

life," says Mrs. Young. "We didn't want her to be alone, so we used to make the boys sit with her. She would have them read the Bible to her.

"She always thought God would return her sight, even though she was in her eighties. She thought her sight would be restored that last Easter she was alive, and when Easter came and she still couldn't see, she cried bitterly. That was the only time her faith wavered."

Andrew and Walter saw their grandmother cry that Easter. They also saw her accept her blindness as God's will and believe in God just as firmly as before. "God's gonna take care of you," she told them again. Dr. and Mrs. Young believed it was a good lesson in faith for their sons, but they did not expect the experience would point either one toward the ministry.

At fifteen, Andrew graduated from high school and entered college. Because he was so young, his parents insisted that he spend his freshman year at a college in New Orleans and live at home.

(COURTESY OF DR. AND MRS. ANDREW J. YOUNG)

2 / A Turning Point

Andrew graduated from Gilbert Academy, a private high school, in 1947 at the age of fifteen. He wanted to go to college in Iowa, but his parents felt he was too young to go so far away from home. They advised him to spend a year at Dillard and to transfer to another college as a sophomore. So Andrew spent his freshman year at Dillard and lived at home.

It was an uneventful year. Because he lived at home, college was not much different from high school to him. He joined the freshman swimming team, studied only enough to get grades that would enable him to transfer to another school, and began to look forward to leaving home and going to college in another state. He still liked the idea of going to college in Iowa, but his parents preferred that he go to Howard University in Washington, D.C.

"My husband was a graduate of Howard," says Mrs. Young, "and we knew some people there who would sort of keep an eye on Andrew. He was only sixteen years old."

If Andrew had a difficult time adjusting to older classmates in elementary and high school, his problems then were nothing compared to those he had at Howard. World War II had ended not long before, and most of the students were veterans whose education was being paid for under the G.I. Bill. Not only were they many years older than Andrew, they were worlds beyond him in experience. Next to them, he felt like a child, and indeed he was little more than a child. He spent his first two years at Howard trying to prove he was a man and did not feel he really belonged until his senior year when he made the swimming and track teams.

It also took him awhile to adjust to living away from home, to doing his own laundry, disciplining himself to study, and budgeting his allowance. He had particular trouble with the last task, although he had a good reason.

"We'd send him an allowance every week, but it would never cover the whole time," his mother recalls. "Then I found out why. His roommate gambled. He'd gamble his own allowance away and then he'd borrow from Andrew, and rarely pay it back. I told Andrew, 'You can't continue lending him money,' but he said, 'Well, I can't go out and eat and see my roommate go hungry.'"

Andrew did not spend much time studying at Howard, where he majored in biology. "I was always reading," he says. "I was always curious. But I was never studying the assignments. My priorities at Howard were a little different from most people's. Most people put partying first, and then school. I always put athletics first, and then partying, and then school." His grades were mediocre, which worried his parents. They wanted him to be able to go to a good medical or dental school. But Andrew did not want to go to medical or dental school. He had no idea what he wanted to do, but he was vaguely dis-

When Andrew graduated from Howard University at nineteen, he was a troubled young man. He had decided he did not want the kind of life his parents planned for him. But he had not decided what he did want.

satisfied with the life he was expected to lead. By the middle of his senior year, he who had enjoyed fraternity parties suddenly saw them as expensive and senseless. His girl friend seemed too interested in material things. The thought of being a dentist and worrying about home mortgages and car payments just did not interest him at all. "Graduation, in particular, was traumatic," he recalls. "Even though I had been through college, I really began doubting that I had learned very much. I suppose I was just typical of your student in those days; you know—gym, girls, the fraternity house and stuff. I also did a lot of sleeping. Suddenly it started to dawn on me that here I was, a college graduate, supposedly, and just what did it all mean? Just where was I going?"

Eventually, he had to tell his parents he had not even sent in applications to any graduate schools.

"I asked him what he wanted to do," his mother says. "He said, 'Well, Mother, I guess I'm going to have to serve in the army sooner or later, so I may as well go and enlist. Maybe after I've served my term in the service I'll know exactly what I want to do.'

"I said, 'Oh, no, Andrew, I don't want you to go into the army. Go on to graduate school for a year and maybe by that time you'll decide what you want to do.'"

Andrew agreed to do as his mother asked, although he thought his parents would be wasting their money. Still, he realized the importance they placed on education. "They saw my education as their responsibility, no matter what the cost."

In late May 1951, Dr. and Mrs. Young drove from New Orleans to Washington, D.C., to pick up their elder son and all his belongings. On the way back, they decided to stop in King's Mountain, North Carolina. A religious camp was operated there every summer and the Youngs knew they could find lodging for the night. "Andrew was assigned a room with a young white minister who was going to Africa," Mrs. Young says, "and Andrew was very impressed with him."

The young man was going to Africa to do missionary work, but he had earned a degree in agriculture so he would not simply be going with a Bible and no helpful skills. He was going to Angola, a country about which Andrew knew because the Congregational Church had a mission there. "In our church, every year we would have an Angola Day and the children were taught that they should share their money and we would send contributions to help the people," says Mrs. Young. "And then sometimes the missionaries would come back and they would come to the church and speak about their work. And Andrew heard all that." Andrew listened as the young minister told him about how he hoped to be able to help the Angolans, and he was impressed by the man's compassion and willingness to give up the physical comforts of life in the United States to travel thousands of miles to Africa. "Here I'd been fighting for two years to prove my manhood and I meet this preacher," Andrew recalls. "He challenged my whole concept of manhood."

He also caused Andrew to re-examine his values. "In all my growing up, through college, nobody ever said to me, 'You've got a responsibility to do something for somebody else.' And I thought to myself, 'Now here's a young white guy going off to Africa to work with my people. This is something I should be doing. It was a judgment on me. If you want to put it in southern language, which I didn't at the time, it was around that experience that I was 'born again.'"

Andrew wanted to get to know the young minister better, so he asked his parents if they could stay on at the camp a few more days. They agreed and stayed four days. "He was very thoughtful after that," his mother recalls. "And when we got home he said, 'Mother, I gave my suit to that fellow because he didn't have one.' He was always doing things like that."

Back home, Andrew met another young minister. The Reverend Nicholas Hood, who was black, had accepted the pastorate of Central Congregational Church and was staying with the Youngs until the parsonage was renovated. Hood would later move to Detroit where he would be pastor of Central Congregational Church there and a member of the Detroit City Council. But back in 1951 he had just graduated from Yale Divinity School.

Andrew resented Hood's presence in the Young home. "My vision of the ministry was not a wholesome one," he explains. "I saw ministers as people who exploited the poor, drove around in Cadillacs, and ate a lot of chicken." But he had to be polite to the new minister of his church, and when Hood asked Andrew to drive to Texas with him, he reluctantly agreed.

Hood had promised to teach a Bible class at a religious camp in Brownsville, Texas, that summer, but he did not want to drive all the way himself. "I won't stay at the camp," said Andrew, "but I'll drive you there and then I'll visit a classmate in San Antonio."

In those days, driving through the South was not a pleasant experience for blacks. They were in constant fear of meeting up with a group of racist whites on some lonely stretch of road. Because whites were rarely prosecuted for committing crimes against blacks, some whites made a sport of attacking defenseless blacks, and an uncomfortably large number of blacks were known to die or disappear mysteriously after they ventured into unfamiliar areas.

"We were kind of nervous driving through those Texas woods to the conference center," Andrew recalls with a chuckle. "We wondered if we were going to find faith or get lynched." But they made the trip safely, and Andrew got to know the young minister better during the drive. He was struck by how much Hood seemed to enjoy his work. "I know it's a cliché," Andrew says, "but he actually seemed to be living his work."

Andrew ended up staying at the camp and not going on to

San Antonio to visit his college friend. When the people at the camp found out that Andrew was a lifeguard, they persuaded him to stay, for they needed a lifeguard. His decision to stay proved to be a turning point in his life.

"It was the first time I'd met any southern white people who were dealing with their own racial training in light of their religious faith," he says. "And I figured if this religion business was powerful enough to overcome hundreds of years of traditional racism, then it must be important; there must be something to it."

The people at the camp were preparing for a major project in the coming year. Called the United Christian Youth Movement, the project's goal was to win a million young people for Christ. They had thirty white volunteers but no black volunteers. Would Andrew be willing to work for six months, without pay, for the Lord? they asked.

"When Andrew came home from the camp, he spoke to me about it," his mother says. "I didn't want him to be out of school because the army might take him. He had been deferred because he was in school, but the Korean War was going on and I was sure he would be drafted. He said, 'Well, if it's the Lord's will that the army take me, so be it, but I want to do this.'

"I didn't know at the time that he was getting interested in being a minister. We just thought he liked working with young people, like he did in our church. Anyway, this was what he wanted to do so we said all right."

Andrew was sent to Indiana for a training course and then assigned to work in Rhode Island and Connecticut. His headquarters were at Hartford Seminary in Hartford, Connecticut. He found the work exhilarating. For the first time, he felt he had a purpose to his life.

"A lot of people crossed my path about that time," Andrew says. In addition to the young white minister he met at King's

Mountain and the Reverend Nicholas Hood, he also met a Yale classmate of Hood's who was going to do missionary work in Rhodesia, and then there were also all the other volunteers in the United Christian Youth Movement. "At that time, I really became interested in Africa, and in the challenge of people giving their lives to others," he says.

On visits home, Andrew talked excitedly about his experiences. "From time to time we had some of the other volunteers staying at our house," Mrs. Young recalls, "and they would talk about Andrew and how impressed they were with him. So I really wasn't surprised when at the end of the six months he called me from Hartford and said, 'Mother, I've decided to stay at the seminary. Will you send me the tuition?'"

Andrew knew his father would be disappointed about his decision, and Dr. Young was. "I tried to tell him about the security and the nice opportunities in the professional field, but he said, 'Well, Daddy, I wouldn't make any money if I went into medicine because if I went into medicine I would go to Africa as a missionary.'"

"I don't think I was as disappointed as my husband was," says Mrs. Young, "but I never thought he would go into the ministry. Maybe if we'd recognized the signs—he was always so generous and wanted to help everybody. But we didn't. As a matter of fact, we thought that Walter would be the one who would be the minister, but Walter is the one who became a dentist!"

The only person close to Andrew who was not surprised about his decision was his friend from childhood, Tom Dent. Dent, who would become a respected poet, had argued with Andrew about religion, among other things, and knew that Andrew had a strong faith. "Andy is the type of person who generates around positives," says Dent. "I ask questions and end up with other questions. Andy asks questions and ends up with answers."

Thus Andrew Young, not quite twenty years old, made one of his major life decisions and chose a life much different from the one his parents had envisioned for him. They had expected him to go on to study medicine and to set up a practice in a southern city, to marry a nice girl like the one he had met at Howard, and to enjoy a good life, respected because of his profession, comfortably well off. Instead, he had chosen to work for other people, hoped to go to Africa to do missionary work or to a small church in some poor rural area of the South. And if he married, he wanted to marry a girl who would be willing to share that kind of life with him. "I was sort of engaged to a girl, a college sweetheart," he says, "but that ended when I chose the ministry."

Andrew entered Hartford Seminary in the winter of 1951–1952, and for the first time in his life he found that he was eager to study. He actually wanted to read assigned books and he read those that were assigned and many more about great philosophers and religious leaders in history. He was particularly impressed by the philosophy and writings of Mohandas Gandhi, who had led the people of India in their struggle for independence from Great Britain. Gandhi taught his people to fight the British without weapons, to disobey British laws, to hold marches and strikes against unfair treatment, but to use no violence. Thousands were beaten and did not fight back. Thousands more were jailed and made no attempt to secure release. Gandhi's first followers were people of the lowest Indian castes, or classes, but as the movement spread people of higher castes joined in.

The British authorities did not know how to control the protesters, who would not fight back and who did not mind going to jail. World opinion turned against the British for fighting against defenseless and passive people. It took seventeen years, but in 1947 Great Britain finally granted independence to India. Gandhi's methods, which he called "passive resistance," had proved more powerful than all the weapons and punishments the British could muster.

Andrew was fascinated by Gandhi's philosophy. It seemed to him that Gandhi had preached what Jesus had—to love your enemy, to turn the other cheek. It also seemed to him that if black people in the United States could have a leader like Mohandas Gandhi, perhaps they could win some of the rights they were denied. He would like to have met Gandhi, but the Indian leader had been assassinated in 1948 by a fanatic Hindu who was against Gandhi's new drive to unite the Hindus and Moslems of India.

At the seminary, Andrew found that he was more comfortable with his white southern classmates than with northern whites or northern blacks. "When I went North to school, black northerners used to poke fun at me for being from the South," he recalls. "It wasn't a racial thing. Once, I was refused a track suit because the coach figured no southern black could run fast enough to make the team." He also found that there was plenty of racism on that side of the Mason-Dixon line. Public transportation and rest rooms were not segregated, nor were most restaurants, but he knew there were hotels and restaurants that would not admit blacks, that most blacks lived segregated from whites, and that they could not get management jobs in white-owned businesses. As a student who was not looking for a job and who did not have the money for exclusive hotels and restaurants, he was not particularly affected by northern racism. He worked out in the gym, dated girls he met in the Hartford area, and though he was far from knowing exactly what he wanted to do with his life, he felt really content for the first time in several years, for now his life had a purpose.

Hartford Seminary required its students to serve some sort of internship each summer, to work in a church or to do the work of the church. Andrew wanted to go to New York to do recreational work with a YMCA program there. At the same time, he figured he could train in track for the Olympics. He knew he was good and he was a great competitor. Trying out for the Olympics was a logical extension of his natural competitiveness. But his mother had other ideas. She didn't want her son 'way up in New York all summer. She wanted him nearer home. Through her church, she learned that the small town of Marion, Alabama, was looking for a summer pastor, so she called her son. "Andrew, there's this little town that really needs a pastor. If you go there, you'll be nearer home," she said. The idea didn't particularly appeal to him, but he finally gave in, and gave up his hopes to do much training for the Olympics that summer.

Among the families in the small Congregational Church parish in Marion were the Childs. Mr. Childs' family operated a bakery on Main Street and Mrs. Childs was a school teacher. Their two sons and three daughters had all grown up in Marion and attended Lincoln School, operated by the Congregational Church. A girl named Coretta Scott had gone to the school with them. By the time Andrew Young accepted the pastorate of the Congregational Church in Marion that summer of 1952, the four oldest Childs children were grown. Jean, the youngest, was finishing her sophomore year at Manchester College in Indiana. Since the church had no parsonage, families were asked to open their homes to the young student minister, and he would spend a week or so with each one.

Jean Young recalls, "My mother told me, 'We have a young student minister who's coming for the summer. He's going to need lots of help with the Vacation Bible School program. Will you help when you're home for the summer?' I said, 'Sure, I'll be glad to help,' but I didn't think much more about it."

Andrew arrived in Marion and learned he would stay with the Childs family first. He liked them immediately, and as he became accustomed to their home, he began to think he might like their youngest daughter, although he had not yet met her. "There was a Senior Life Saver certificate on the wall, and a Revised Standard version of the New Testament, underlined, and from the books in her library I could see that we shared many interests," Andrew recalls. "I had become pretty disillusioned with black middle-class women, and at the time I was seriously considering celibacy [not marrying at all]. But these were the things I'd been looking for in a woman—athletically inclined, some religious commitment. I decided the Lord had sent me to Marion to get a wife!"

By that time, Jean had left Manchester College and was visiting her brother, who owns a service station in Tuskeegee, Alabama. The Childs were very impressed with the young student minister, and they decided their daughter should come home to help him immediately, so they drove over to get her. She and Andrew met while he was still staying at her home. He thought she was pretty and just as nice as he had hoped. Jean remembers, "I thought he looked like a clean-cut young man—with very large ears! We were immediately attracted to each other and we worked very closely that summer and a romance grew out of that."

The Childs were very happy about the relationship between their daughter and Andrew and treated him like part of the family. In turn, he acted like part of the family. He loved to tease Mrs. Childs, and with affectionate exasperation she remembers that he would tease her at the most inopportune times. "Near the end of the summer his parents came up for the weekend because they wanted to hear him preach. They stayed with us. We were just sitting down to eat when Andrew came to the table and said to me, 'Oh, I see you've gotten out all your good silver and china. I'm the preacher and when I come I have to eat out of the spaghetti pan.'"

When the summer ended, Andrew went back to Hartford

Seminary and Jean went back to Manchester College, but they corresponded and visited each other at holidays. They had long talks about what they wanted to do with their lives. Andrew spoke of missionary work in Africa and Jean, who was studying for a degree in education, thought she could be of service there, too. Although Jean wanted to finish college first, they agreed that they would get married after her graduation.

The following summer, 1953, Andrew went to Austria to work in a camp for refugees from eastern Europe operated by the Congregational Church. "It was my first international experience," he recalls, "and I liked it." He was very eager to do missionary work in Africa, and that fall both he and Jean made application to go to Angola the next year to work in the Congregational Church-operated mission there. They had learned that one of the black missionaries there was about to retire, so they felt they had a good chance. But it was not to be.

"Somehow," Jean Young recalls, "the people in charge of the mission missed the fact that the two of us were going to get married. We were initially rejected because we were single. By the time they understood that we were going to get married —that we had gotten married—we were involved in other things. Also, by the time they offered to send us, the Portuguese government in Angola was beginning to expel missionaries, and there would have been problems anyway."

Andrew Young and Jean Childs were married on June 7, 1954, after she graduated from Manchester College. Andrew still had another semester to complete at Hartford Seminary, but they decided not to wait any longer. Since the possibility of their being sent to Angola seemed dim, Andrew accepted a summer pastorate in a tiny church in Thomasville, Georgia.

"We went down there immediately after we were married," says Jean Young. "It was a sort of city-country parish. He was pastor of two Congregational churches, the little church in

Andrew Young and Jean Childs were married June 7, 1954. They looked forward to a life as minister and wife in a church in a small southern town.

(COURTESY OF DR. AND MRS. ANDREW J. YOUNG)

Thomasville and another one in Beachton, about fifteen miles away. And we lived in this big old two-story parsonage that hadn't housed a minister in years and years. So we sort of went in with hammers and nails and put up sheet rock and tile and did whatever we could to make it livable again."

It was a very poor parish, for the blacks in Thomasville and especially Beachton were mostly laborers and sharecroppers, if they were lucky enough to have work at all. Some lived miles away from the churches, and going to church on Sunday was a big event. It was an opportunity for them to see their friends, for those who worked to relax, for those who were unemployed to forget their troubles. The young student minister soon learned that his new parishioners were somewhat different from the people he was accustomed to. "Any time I'd pause during my sermon, some old sister would start a new hymn and it would be fifteen minutes before I could get back to what I was saying," he recalls with a chuckle. "Or I'd work real hard on a sermon and they'd be saying so many 'Amens' and 'Tell the Truths' that I'd get so worked up I'd forget what I'd written and just go on and preach!"

Despite the frustrations, Andrew felt challenged in Thomasville and Beachton. The summer ended too quickly for him. He did not feel he had done enough. That tiny, poor parish needed him. Jean agreed. They went back to Hartford so Andrew could complete his studies. They rented a small apartment near the seminary and Jean got a job teaching third grade in a local school. Six months later, in February 1955, Andrew Young graduated from Hartford Seminary with a Bachelor of Divinity degree and was ordained in the Congregational Church.* The minister who charged him told him that if he wanted to be an effective minister he should keep his bags

---

* In 1957, most Congregational churches joined with the Evangelical and Reformed Church to form the United Church of Christ.

Andrew is ordained. The minister at his ordination told him that if he wanted to be an effective minister he should be ready to face constant danger.

(COURTESY OF DR. AND MRS. ANDREW J. YOUNG)

packed, because to be an effective minister was to be in constant danger of being run out of town. With this warning in mind, Andrew and Jean Young returned to Georgia. The time they spent there would prove an educational experience, especially for Andrew. Brought up in the middle class, never having lived in poverty, before the preceding summer he had been unaware of the kind of life that blacks in Thomasville and Beachton lived. "I wanted to be around plain, wise black folk," he recalls. "It was where I reclaimed my roots, where I began to develop racial identity and an appreciation of black culture."

3 / Activist Minister

"Thomasville was one of those southern towns that served primarily as a resort for northerners," says Jean Young. "They would come down and buy these old plantations and spend two or three weeks a year at them, hunting quail. And that kind of situation generated a certain level of complacency among the black residents. They didn't feel as strongly about segregation as some of the people in other communities, and yet the discrepancies between the blacks and the whites were so obvious."

Perhaps one reason the black residents of Thomasville did not seem to resent segregation was that the majority of them were either very old or very young. "Sixty percent were under eighteen," says Andrew. "The adults would go North to work and send the kids back down South to live with their grandparents, and it seemed that the kids needed someone to work with them. So we cleared playgrounds and built basketball courts and I took them to conferences and to colleges and did for the entire community the things that my parents had done for me."

The young people responded to Andrew and Jean. They were not like any other minister and wife they'd ever known. Jean remembers with a laugh that she and her husband were kind of hard for the adults in Thomasville to figure out. "We were both young. I wore shorts and he played basketball with the kids, and the local Baptist ministers really came down hard on Andrew. In the southern Baptist tradition, wives don't go around in shorts and young couples don't go out dancing and that kind of thing. We were so involved in the community and Andrew was extremely dedicated, and yet there was criticism, and rumblings from the more staid ministers about how a minister was supposed to behave."

To Andrew and Jean, the concerns of the other ministers seemed petty when there were so many real problems to worry about. "Alcoholism, unemployment, pre-teen pregnancy—all the problems of society were concentrated in this little tiny church," Jean says, "and Andrew began to realize *very* soon that he could not solve their problems without looking at the situation in the total community. He became involved in a very *staid* organization called the Business and Civic League and was elected president of it, and he decided that the nice, civic-minded thing to do was to register people to vote."

Very few blacks in the South voted in those days, especially in the rural areas. Some did not even realize that, as American citizens, they were supposed to be able to. The southern white power structure had kept black people from voting in a variety of ways. One was to threaten them with violence or losing their jobs. Another was to charge a poll tax. Poll taxes were usually only one or two dollars a year, but most poor southern blacks could not afford to pay them. Still another way was to require prospective voters to pass a literacy test, and since many southern blacks could not read, they could not pass the test.

Andrew Young began to talk to his congregations in Thomasville and Beachton about the importance of voting. Through the Business and Civic League, he raised funds to pay the poll taxes and organized volunteers to teach prospective voters to read and to answer the questions they might be asked on the literacy test.

The idea of registering more black people as voters seemed a simple and natural one to Andrew Young, but to many whites in the area it was neither simple nor natural. In fact, it was downright subversive. If black people had the vote, they might elect black officials, or turn down proposed laws that were designed to benefit whites and not blacks. In short, it would give them a measure of power, and the last thing these whites wanted was for blacks to have any kind of power. Blacks in other southern communities had found that out in tragic ways. In 1955 the Reverend George W. Lee of Belzoni, Mississippi, had managed to get about thirty blacks to register to vote. In May 1955 he had been shot and killed. No one had been arrested for the crime. Also in the early 1950s, a man named Lamar Smith was active in getting people to register in Brookhaven, Mississippi. He too was shot and killed, and again no one had been brought to justice. Many similar incidents had happened throughout the South, but people were not inclined to talk about them, and the press gave little coverage to the killing of blacks in those days. Andrew Young, who was largely unfamiliar with the way things were in the rural South, was unaware of how greatly he might disturb the social status quo in Thomasville, Georgia, by trying to get black people to register to vote.

The local chapter of the Ku Klux Klan was particularly disturbed by Andrew's activities. The organization had been started after the Civil War by white southerners who felt that blacks should never have been freed from slavery. A secret organization, whose members always went to meetings and other Klan activities dressed in hooded white robes, the Klan had made a business of frightening black people, sometimes by committing violent acts like beatings and lynchings, and sometimes by holding demonstrations where they burned crosses on black people's lawns to warn them against stepping out of their "place" as second-class citizens. This voter registration idea was considered an example of blacks trying to step out of their place. The Ku Klux Klan decided to stage a march against the uppity minister Young and his supporters.

"It was our first intimate experience with the Klan," says Jean Young. "Of course, if you grow up black in the South you know about the Klan. Your parents tell you stories and you hear of others' experiences. But we were so young, and I guess somewhat naïve, that we were more curious than anything else. We went out to see the demonstration because we wanted to see the *hoods* and all the other regalia! It was a novelty to us. But after we got home we had a very serious discussion. We had a young baby and we discussed the implications for our family and what taking action represented."

The older residents of Thomasville also had to think seriously about the implications of their actions, for they knew people who lost their jobs or were beaten because they tried to register. Try as they might, the Youngs could not seem to get a movement going, and they both realized it would be risking their lives to try to carry the burden alone. The situation lacked the ingredients necessary for a spontaneous grassroots movement, but the Youngs continued their voting rights drive.

Andrew and Jean knew that a movement for black people's rights was possible, because it had happened in Montgomery, Alabama. There, in December 1955, a black woman named

Rosa Parks had refused to give up her seat on a city bus to a white man and had been arrested. The incident angered members of Montgomery's black community and a group of black ministers had formed a committee to organize a boycott of the buses by the city's blacks. A young minister named Martin Luther King, Jr., who happened to be married to Coretta Scott from Marion, Alabama, was named president of the organization, which was called the Montgomery Improvement Association. Like Andrew Young, he too had been impressed by the philosophy and writings of Mohandas Gandhi and he called the boycott a nonviolent protest against segregation on the buses.

The city authorities and individual white citizens tried everything they could to end the boycott. There was violence, Klan night rides, King's home was bombed. But the blacks did not fight back. Partly because they were sick of segregation but mostly because they could understand and act based on the concept of nonviolence, particularly with ministers leading them, the black people of Montgomery did not give in. It was the first time in anyone's memory that black people had really stuck together.

The boycott attracted national press coverage, and as the rest of the country saw the white violence against nonviolent blacks, public opinion was won over to the boycotters' cause. Just over a year after the boycott began, the United States Supreme Court declared segregation on Montgomery's buses unconstitutional.

Like other southern blacks who were interested in bringing about change, Andrew Young had followed news reports of the Montgomery bus boycott closely and been very impressed with the courage and the nonviolent philosophy of Martin Luther King. Unlike many other southern blacks, he had an opportunity to meet King in his home, through his wife and King's.

"Coretta Scott King came from Marion, Alabama," says Jean

Young, "and she and one of my older sisters were close, so we knew the Scott family well. Andrew was very interested in meeting Martin because he had heard so much about him, and so it was very natural that they should meet. We visited them one time when we were passing through Montgomery on our way to Marion. I really didn't know Martin, but I knew Coretta very well, so we just stopped by and visited them. It was a very nice, low-keyed, get-acquainted meeting, but Andrew and Martin immediately related to each other."

Andrew Young says, "We talked a few times after that and I volunteered to help. But nothing much happened."

The success of the boycott caused King and others in the Montgomery Improvement Association to feel that other racial barriers could be lifted through similar methods, not just in Montgomery but in other parts of the South as well. Other southern black ministers agreed, and in January 1957, at a conference of black ministers in Atlanta, Georgia, the Southern Christian Leadership Conference (SCLC) was formed to urge the federal government to pass civil rights laws and to promote the movement for black equality in the South. King was elected its president. Among the other founders of the SCLC were the Reverend Ralph David Abernathy, another Montgomery minister who had participated in the bus boycott with King, the Reverend Fred Shuttlesworth of Birmingham, and Reverend Hosea Williams, a former chemist with the U.S. Department of Agriculture [he was not a minister, but tacked the "Reverend" onto his name because he found it helped him in organizing southern blacks to fight segregation]. The Reverend Andrew Young was not at the meeting.

Meanwhile, a much older organization, the National Association for the Advancement of Colored People (NAACP) had been working toward ending segregation, but more quietly and slowly, through the courts. In 1954, NAACP lawyers had brought about a Supreme Court decision that had declared segregated schools unconstitutional. The Court declared that the states should proceed "with all deliberate speed" to desegregate their schools. The trouble was, the Court did not define what "deliberate speed" was, and many states decided to take their time about desegregating their schools. Still, the Court's decision had been a step forward.

The decade of the 1950s would see a slow but real change in the government's attitude toward its black citizens. In 1957 Congress passed, and President Dwight D. Eisenhower signed into law, the first federal civil rights bill since 1875. It created a Civil Rights Commission to look into voting irregularities, and authorized the Department of Justice to send out court injunctions to southern states where poll taxes were charged and literacy tests were required. Unfortunately, it was not a very strong law. It was designed to mollify civil rights activists by showing them that the government was doing *something.* But it was also designed not to anger unduly the southern legislators who were absolutely against federal intervention in the affairs of their states. The commission created by the bill was not given enough power to do much about voter registration irregularities. Black people were still denied the right to register to vote, and their appeals to the Civil Rights Commission rarely brought help. King and the SCLC tried to get a voting rights drive started, but the sense of commitment, of unity and driving purpose, that had characterized the Montgomery bus boycott, was lacking.

Southern black people were more interested in things that affected their everyday lives, like segregated buses. As the Youngs had found out in Thomasville, many southern blacks did not realize the importance of voting. They did not believe they could exercise power by the ballot.

By late 1957, Andrew Young was feeling restless. He had believed the people in Thomasville and Beachton were basically different from his family and the other middle-class black people he knew. He had thought that because they were so close to the basics of life, they understood life better and this understanding would remain with them no matter how their economic or social situation changed. He had read the writings of Karl Marx, a German philosopher whose theories formed the basis for communism, and agreed with the part of Marx's philosophy which held that people of the lower classes, if they could unite, could be a stronger force than the upper classes, could take over society and create a new one, a fairer society where everyone would have enough and everyone would be equal.

Andrew Young believed that if people like the poor black people of Thomasville, Georgia, exercised the power of their numbers and gained control, they would not be money-hungry like the middle class, but would want everyone to have an adequate income. They would not look down on other people as the middle class did, but would want everyone to be treated equally. He believed that they would somehow be "better" people than those of higher classes. After a few years in Georgia, he realized he had been mistaken. As he recalls, "I think that I went to the South with a romanticized view that the world would be saved by the poor, who knew suffering and love and God. After three years, I realized that all the poor wanted to be was middle class. I realized that class analysis, like racial analysis, doesn't work."

Thus, when the National Council of Churches approached him about going to their headquarters in New York City to work with their Department of Youth, he listened to the offer with an open mind. When Jean learned of the offer, she was not in favor of it. She liked Thomasville, liked her teaching job, and was reluctant to leave the warmth and neighborliness of small-town southern black society. But Andrew was somewhat frustrated as a southern small-town preacher. The new job would give him more opportunities to reach many more people. After a great deal of prayer and thought, he decided to accept the job.

Andrew and Jean Young and their two small daughters, Andrea and Lisa, moved to New York and settled in the borough of Queens. Their third daughter, Paula, was born there. Jean did not get a teaching job but instead enrolled at Queens College and earned her master's degree in education. She was not particularly happy in Queens. "Some of my children's first negative racial experiences occurred out in Queens when they were three, four, and five years old," she recalls. But she was willing to make some sacrifice for her husband as he embarked on his new career.

At the headquarters of the National Council of Churches, Andrew Young was not at all surprised to find that out of the entire staff he was the only non-white and that, in addition to youth relations, he was assigned to race relations. In those days, blacks were "ghettoized" in that way, but Andrew decided to do the best job he could. He brought great energy and many new ideas to his work, and for the first time the National Council of Churches staff began really to concentrate on young people and on how to reach them through their own culture.

Perhaps because he had not so long before felt his life had no purpose, Young felt keenly the alienation and loneliness that young people experienced because they lacked commitment to anything. He remembered how he had felt when he met the young minister who was going to Angola to do missionary work, and how meeting the young man had caused him to question his values and his concept of manhood. He had been changed, and he hoped he might in turn help other young people find something to which to commit themselves. It seemed to him that there was so much energy out there that could be channeled to a good purpose. Had he worked with more black youth, one of the good purposes he would have emphasized particularly would have been African development and independence. While he was in New York, he had the opportunity to see Tom Mboya, a Kenyan who was working for the independence of his country, and he could not help but compare that young man with black youth in the United States. "There was Mboya, twenty-seven or twenty-eight years old, leading his country to freedom. And here were America's Negro students, about the same age, jivin' and assimilatin'." Although he worked almost exclusively with white youths, he still stressed the development in them of a world view and during his time in New York often led youth groups to the United Nations and to Washington to lobby for foreign aid to newly independent African countries.

As the associate director of the department of youth work, Young was in charge of the Council's athletics and media programs. He inaugurated an NCC-sponsored television series called "Look Up and Live" aimed directly at youthful viewers, for he recognized the importance of television as a way to reach young people. The youthful-looking Andrew Young was the host of the series, and in those days he was one of the few blacks to be seen on television in any capacity. Blacks did not do commercials then, or star in their own series. But Andrew Young hosted a television program every Sunday morning. It was, in his opinion, a very valuable experience. "It introduced me to the area of mass media and gave me an appreciation of the methods and the values of modern communication," he says. "That experience was tremendously helpful when I got to the civil rights movement."

The civil rights movement, meanwhile, was beginning to emerge. Deciding to use the Civil Rights Act of 1957 for whatever it was worth, the SCLC led marches and organized voter registration drives, but it was two students at North Carolina Agricultural and Technical College in Greensboro, who thought they ought to be able to eat at the local Woolworth's

lunch counter, who really accelerated the civil rights movement. The two students sat down at the lunch counter and
refused to leave unless they were served. They sat for several
days and were not served, but no police action was taken
against them. News of the action spread by word-of-mouth,
and on the fourth day some students at the white Women's
College of the University of North Carolina joined the black
students. Naturally, that action was reported in the local newspapers. It was read by black and white students in colleges in
Durham, North Carolina, and they started a sit-in at a local
restaurant. Within two weeks, college students in four neighboring states had begun their own sit-ins, and a month later
ten southern states were involved. Worried over the rapid
growth of the student movement, the authorities began to re-
taliate. Students were arrested and treated roughly, but they
did not fight back. They followed the same nonviolent principles that had been employed in the Montgomery bus boycott. Seeing defenseless fellow students treated in this manner,
other students were spurred to action. A real, spontaneous,
grassroots movement had begun.

The SCLC invited the sit-in leaders of all ten affected states
to an organizational rally at Shaw University in Raleigh, North
Carolina, and at that rally in April 1960 the Student Nonviolent Coordinating Committee (SNCC) was born. Although
it was separate from the SCLC, its goals were similar, and Martin Luther King, Jr., was invited to be its adviser.

Perhaps in response to this evidence of a growing movement
for black civil rights, President Eisenhower signed into law a
second Civil Rights Bill in May 1960. It was another law that
was too weak to be effective, but it served to show southern
blacks that their activities were not being ignored, that they
were having some influence.

Reading newspapers and watching news reports on television, Andrew and Jean Young followed all this activity oc-

curring in their native area of the country. Working so closely with young people, Andrew could see ways the southern students could be inspired and counseled more effectively, and from time to time he wrote and made suggestions to King and other friends who were active in the movement. Imperceptibly, both he and Jean were being drawn to the South and to all that was happening down there.

By 1961 much was happening. Sit-ins at lunch counters spread across the South, and so did violence by the authorities. In April 1961, leaders of SCLC and another veteran civil rights group, the Congress of Racial Equality (CORE), met with the leaders of SNCC and decided that interstate buses would be the next target for integration. Members of the organizations would stage "Freedom Rides" through the South and at every stop desegregate the bus station dining rooms and restroom facilities. The first two buses set out from Washington, D.C., on May 4. By the time they reached Alabama, the rides had been well publicized and waiting crowds beat the riders savagely. The beatings only served to increase media coverage of the Freedom Rides. Every night the Youngs sat glued to their television set, watching the evening news. "Then the Nashville Story came on," says Andrew.

The reference is to the impromptu Freedom Ride that John Lewis, executive director of SNCC, and a group of other sit-in veterans began in Nashville, Tennessee. After the violent confrontations of the organized Freedom Rides, Attorney General Robert Kennedy had requested a "cooling-off" period, and CORE had canceled the Freedom Ride that had been scheduled to originate from Nashville. Lewis and the others believed that if the Ride did not take place, the segregationists would think that they could defeat the civil rights movement by violence, so they bought tickets to Birmingham and announced they were going to make the Ride anyway. In Birmingham, they were arrested and jailed, but when they were released they went to the bus station to buy tickets to Montgomery. As the bus pulled into the station in Montgomery, the Freedom Riders got a kind of eerie feeling. No one seemed to be around, and that was not normal. The bus driver opened the door and walked away from the bus. Then the mob descended. Five or six hundred white men attacked the Freedom Riders with ax handles and chains, beating them senseless.

As Andrew and Jean Young recall, "We sat there in the comfort of our Queens home watching kids get their heads beaten in, and we looked at each other and asked, 'Why are we here? What are we doing up here?' And then we said to each other, 'Let's go back South. That's where we belong.'"

4 / "The Lord Will Take Care of Us"

Fortunately, just about the time Andrew and Jean Young decided they should return to the South, Andrew was offered a job that would enable them to do so. The United Church of Christ had received funding from the Field Foundation to operate a voter registration drive, whose headquarters would be in Alabama. Andrew was appointed director of the project. Late in 1961 the Youngs moved to Atlanta, Georgia, because they liked that city and because it had a sizable black population. Andrew's younger brother, Walter, had moved there with his family. Martin Luther King, Jr., and his family had also moved there, in 1960.

Dr. and Mrs. Young were not particularly happy about the move. Of course, they wanted to have Andrew and Jean and the children back in the South, but they were fearful that

Andrew was going to be in for trouble if he got involved in the civil rights struggle. Mrs. Young recalls how she felt when Andrew told her he was joining the movement. "When he called me to tell me about it, I said, 'Oh, no, Andrew. You're gonna give up a job with the National Council of Churches and go down *there*, not knowing if you're going to be able to *survive*? It isn't just your own safety you've got to think about, but the safety of your children.' He said. 'Don't worry. God's gonna take care of us. Just continue praying.' Well, I stayed on my knees praying *all* the time. The Protestant church wasn't open all the time, so I went to the Catholic Church every day."

Dr. Young was equally concerned with the safety of Andrew and his family. He says, "I was always off-balance, because I knew the habits and customs in the South."

Andrew understood his parents' fears. At the same time, he believed he had to take the risks. Not yet thirty years old, he was part of a different generation. As he once explained, "My grandfather, a successful small-business man, wanted financial independence. My father, using my grandfather's money, pushed for education; he saw that as a more permanent defense against racism than money. My generation, when its time for decision came, saw neither of those as a defense. It began to think in community terms, in terms of advancing on a broad political and cultural and economic front."

The odds against that kind of advancement for southern blacks in 1961 were long indeed. The movement was still a small one, and it could not count many victories. Blacks in Montgomery, Alabama, were no longer segregated on city buses; blacks in most southern college cities were no longer refused service at department store luncheonettes; but life had really not changed very much. The SCLC and other organizations did not have broad-based support or much money. But they had to start somewhere, and in Andrew Young's opinion, getting black people registered to vote so they could exercise what should have been their unquestioned right to vote as citizens seemed the logical place.

As in Thomasville, Georgia, Young found that the drive he had been appointed to direct had to be conducted on the most basic levels, "teaching people how to spell, teaching them what a mayor did and how he affected their lives." Young showed great sensitivity to the needs of the people the drive was trying to reach, and great organizational skill in addressing the needs both of the people and of the drive. At the same time, he contributed a variety of ideas to the SCLC, and it was not long before he joined that organization.

At that time, the SCLC was still pretty conservative. It had, for example, withdrawn its support of the Freedom Rides when white reaction against them had become too violent. The young militants of SNCC had kept sending more riders to be beaten up, however, and at last the Administration of President John F. Kennedy had sent federal troops to escort the buses and to protect the riders from further violence. The SNCC leaders had felt triumphant, but SCLC leaders and leaders of CORE failed to see the federal action as positive. What was the progress when a handful of Freedom Riders needed 400 soldiers to protect them as they rode through the South? And what kind of movement was it that engaged the active participation of so few people? The average black person was not willing to go on a Freedom Ride. Clearly, the average black was not even willing to engage in much safer actions. The civil rights struggle might be receiving a lot of publicity, but it represented only a small percentage of the nation's black people; fewer than one million of the twenty-two million blacks in the United States were participating.

Early in November 1961, the Interstate Commerce Commission had ruled against segregation on all interstate vehicles and public facilities. The ruling was obviously a direct response to the Freedom Rides, and the kind of "confrontation politics" the leaders of SNCC favored. Although they had to admit such tactics appeared to work, the leaders of the SCLC could not bring themselves to approve them. They pointed out that the ICC ruling was being ignored just as the Supreme Court school desegregation decision and the two Civil Rights Acts were not being upheld. Most of the SCLC leaders were in favor of more conservative action, like voter registration drives, when Andrew Young joined the organization.

It is widely believed that at that time King and the SCLC were desperate to regain control of the movement from militants like the leaders of SNCC. That is not true, according to Andrew Young. "I don't know of a single instance where SCLC decided in Atlanta that it was going to start a movement. In every case it was the local people getting into difficulty and coming to us to help them get out." Civil rights groups in Albany, Georgia, had gotten together and decided to campaign for the desegregation of all public facilities there. The impetus had come in December 1961 when SNCC workers had decided to test the new ICC ruling as it applied to the Georgia Central Railroad. They had been arrested, and local civil rights groups had rallied to their cause, demanding the desegregation of all public facilities in the city. Dr. W. G. Anderson, the leader of the Albany groups, believed that in order to succeed, the Albany movement had to have the public support of the SCLC and, in particular, Martin Luther King. The SNCC leaders disagreed, but Anderson prevailed. In the recollection of Andrew Young, King was simply asked to speak for one night in Albany:

"And so Martin went to speak in Albany and got to preachin' and going on, and the folk were very excited about it all, and there were two churches packed and people all out in the street, and then Dr. Anderson got up and announced, 'Be back in the morning at nine o'clock and bring your marching shoes, and Dr. King is going to march with us.' "

There was not much King could do but join the march, and he was jailed along with the rest of the demonstrators. That, according to Young, got the SCLC into "confrontation politics." King was released in a few days and the Albany authorities made some small concessions to the black community. History will not record Albany, Georgia, as a major civil rights milestone, but in a way it was, for it got the SCLC involved in the confrontation movement, not by design but almost by accident. For the next few years Martin Luther King and Andrew Young and the others in SCLC would not so much orchestrate civil rights activity as respond to it, and try to keep it under control.

King had been released from the jail in Albany after an "anonymous donor" had paid his fine, and he was criticized for not remaining in jail and suffering for his beliefs. In Andrew Young's recollection, that criticism bothered King, and he was also troubled by the movement of the civil rights struggle toward confrontation tactics. "I think after Albany he went through a period where he was trying to decide whether even to continue or not." King had not been in Atlanta, or served as pastor of Ebenezer Baptist Church long, and as Young recalls, he could have been quite happy pastoring that church, writing books, and lecturing. For a few months he concentrated on those activities, and by early 1963 Young and others in SCLC were worrying that he would forsake the civil rights movement altogether. This, they felt, could not be allowed. He was a natural leader, he had charisma, he *had* to lead the movement. Andrew Young says, "It seemed to be Randolph Blackwell, Dorothy Cotton, and James Bevel and myself meeting out at Blackwell's house late at night trying to figure out what we ought to do and scheme up on Martin to try to get him to lead it. I'm convinced that Martin never wanted to be a leader. I mean, everything he did he was pushed into."

The movement in Birmingham, Alabama, was a case in

point. Early in 1963 the Reverend Fred Shuttlesworth, a founder of SCLC, approached the other leaders of the organization. As Young recalls, "He said they just had to do something about Birmingham, and they were going to do it with or without our help, but they'd like us to come over and help them organize it."

There was no question something had to be done about Birmingham, which was one of the most segregated of southern cities and which had taken no steps to change the situation in light of civil rights activity elsewhere. Restaurants that wanted black business as well as white were required to have two entrances, marked "Colored" and "White," and inside a wall at least seven feet tall to separate the two races. In 1951 a new black resident of the city found on the statute books a city ordinance that prohibited blacks and whites from playing checkers together! Over a period of years there had been close to fifty "unsolved" bombings of black homes and institutions. The leaders of the SCLC decided that if they could have enough time to organize demonstrations and take steps to prevent violence, a campaign in Birmingham might work.

By that time Andrew Young had become one of the inner circle of SCLC leaders. He was a superb organizer, and he had another talent that the other leaders recognized as valuable: he was very successful dealing with white people. He did not distrust white people because they were white, as many did, but realized that if a mutual interest could be found, whites could be negotiated with. King realized the Birmingham campaign, to be successful, would have to involve negotiation with the city's white leaders. Young was given the chief responsibility for planning and directing the campaign.

Plans for the demonstrations were drawn up in secret, but officials of the Kennedy Administration were informed beforehand. Birmingham was a die-hard segregationist town, and Young and the others wanted to be sure they could count on federal assistance if they needed it. At organizational meetings in black Birmingham churches, people who planned to take part in the demonstrations were schooled in the tenets of non-violence, urged to refrain from violence of "fist, tongue and heart," and asked to sign a pledge to go to prison if need be.

The demonstrations began in April. They started quietly and on a small scale with student sit-ins in a few downtown lunch counters, for Andrew Young realized that any massive demonstrations would invite massive resistance. He also wanted to attract more of Birmingham's blacks to the cause and knew that many would be frightened off if there were any violence. Gradually the number of demonstrations and peaceful marches increased. The police responded by making peaceful arrests, for the situation seemed one that could be handled without extreme measures. But as the number of people participating in the demonstrations grew, so did the authorities' concern. Young tried arranging some meetings with white leaders to talk about the situation. One was held at the Church of the Advent in Birmingham. Andrew Young, Fred Shuttlesworth, and a few spokesmen for the city's black community met with a group of white leaders. But right at the start it was clear to the blacks that the meeting was doomed. The whites were so concerned that the rest of Birmingham's whites would find out they had actually met with the blacks that they had insisted on absolute secrecy. And when one of them opened the discussion with, "Tell me, what is it that you niggers want?" the blacks realized little would be accomplished. Nothing was.

At length, the city authorities obtained a court injunction against King and the SCLC and the marchers. If they did not stop the demonstrations, there would be appropriate retaliation and SCLC leaders would be arrested. King, Young and most of the others in SCLC realized that if they obeyed the court injunction they would halt the momentum of the campaign. They held a meeting to tell their followers that they planned to disobey the injunction.

Naturally, some people were concerned about what might happen. They feared that the city's police would feel that the injunction gave them license to do whatever they wanted and would take violent action. Young tried to allay their fears. "The Lord will take care of us," he assured them.

Jean Young recalls, "They used to kid him because he was always saying that: The Lord's gonna take care of it. It became sort of a joke. People would say, 'Check with Andrew, because he's in touch with the Lord.'" But though they laughed about it, the people in the forefront of the civil rights movement needed Andrew Young's optimism. They were venturing into hostile territory, the kind of territory that was white-run Birmingham in the spring of 1963.

The day after the meeting, Martin Luther King joined the Birmingham marchers for the first time. He was arrested and jailed. He hoped that by going to jail he would inspire other clergymen, black and white, to join the campaign. He was disappointed. As he once wrote, "The ultimate tragedy is not the brutality of the bad people but the silence of the good people."

With King in jail and the city's clergymen unwilling to support them, Young and the others realized that they must keep the campaign going. But they were beginning to worry about lack of personnel. So Andrew Young, James Bevel, Dorothy Cotton, and Bernard Lee, who had joined the SCLC in 1960 when King had moved to Atlanta and become King's personal aide and traveling companion, began visiting area colleges and high schools and inviting the students to attend meetings at the black churches after school.

The young people's response was overwhelming, and as word spread, even younger children volunteered. Once, six very small children presented themselves as volunteers before Andrew Young. He told them they were too young to go to jail. He suggested that they go to the library. "You won't get arrested there, but you might learn something," he said. So the children marched off to the nearest white library, made for the children's room, and sat down to read some books. The whites at the library were aghast, but they made no move to evict the children, who in their own way had struck a blow for freedom by integrating the children's room of a white library.

Early one Thursday afternoon a few days later, some one thousand young people gathered at the Sixteenth Street Baptist Church. After receiving instructions from King, who had been released from jail by that time, they dispersed in small groups and casually made their way downtown where they planned to assemble for a march. By the time the police realized that the apparently unconnected groups of laughing, skipping kids were converging in the same area, the groups had begun to connect and the march had started. A thousand children were marching solemnly through downtown Birmingham. Seemingly unaware of the reporters and television cameras that had been rushed to the scene, police clubbed some of the older boys, and roughly hauled hundreds into their waiting vans. The news media recorded it all, for this "children's crusade" in Birmingham was quite a story.

More than a thousand children showed up at the Sixteenth Street Baptist Church the next morning, some of them no more than seven or eight years old. But this time Sheriff Eugene "Bull" Connor was ready for them. He sent police and firemen to surround the church and prevent the children from going downtown. As the children emerged from the exits of the church, fire hoses were turned on them. The powerful streams of water smashed small bodies against fences and to the sidewalks. And amid the screaming and crying, "Bull" Connor ordered his men to release their dogs, who rushed at the children, snarling and snapping, dragging them about like bones. Television cameras were again on hand to record it all, and that night in their living rooms Americans were treated to a sight they would never forget: small children, their clothing drenched and hair matted from the fire hoses, trying in panic to get away from ferocious dogs. Satellites carried the television pictures around the world. Birmingham, Alabama, became an international scandal.

Andrew Young knew it was time to contact Roger Blough again. The executive of U.S. Steel, which was tied in with Tennessee Coal and Iron, which had a major interest in coal-rich Birmingham, would be concerned about the city's image and eager for a settlement. Through Blough, Young was able to make contact with about 100 of Birmingham's white business and financial leaders. No one was using the word "nigger" now. Birmingham's reputation was at stake, and its industries could suffer. Three days after the hoses and dogs were set on Birmingham's black children, a biracial agreement was announced whereby public accommodations would be desegregated, job opportunities increased, and all those arrested in the demonstrations would be freed.

The next day, bombs were thrown at Martin Luther King's hotel room and at the home of his brother A. D. King. In retaliation, blacks who were sick of hearing the philosophy of nonviolence set fire to white homes and stores and smashed police cars. King, Young and others walked through black neighborhoods pleading for an end to the violence, and it subsided as quickly as it had begun. It did not mar the over-all impact of the Birmingham campaign, and indeed that campaign proved to be a major milestone in the civil rights movement. It was certainly one impetus to President Kennedy's nationally televised call to the country in June to fulfill its promise of freedom and equality and to the Congress to pass a civil rights bill that would be really effective.

The leaders of SCLC decided to capitalize on the President's commitment and on the victory in Birmingham by staging a march on Washington, D.C. Andrew Young was once again in charge of planning and organization—a considerable task, given the number of people the march would involve and the amount of money it would take. Despite the seeming financial strength of the SCLC, Young recalls that the organization in those days had neither a strong financial nor a strong organizational base: "We never had a budget to do what we decided to do. We decided to do something and went on out and did it on a kind of faith that money to do it would come." Young had to think about a lot of logistical matters in planning that kind of march. They hoped to have at least a hundred thousand people. They would have to be lodged somewhere, and fed—and just where were they all going to go to the bathroom? And how would the march be kept peaceful with all those people?

Somehow, the money came, and the people to help, and the spirit to make it all work. The August 1973 March on Washington was one of the happiest, most peaceful demonstrations the nation's capital has ever seen. There was a spirit of hope in the air, a spirit underscored by the theme of Martin Luther King's speech at the Lincoln Memorial that day. "I have a dream . . . ," he began, and by the time he was finished there were few people in that crowd of 200,000 whose eyes were dry and who did not think King's dream could come true. Up there with King, Andrew Young thanked God that he was able to be part of it.

A little over two weeks later a bomb exploded during Bible class at Birmingham's Sixteenth Street Baptist Church and killed four little black girls. It was the kind of senseless violence that sickened both blacks and most whites. It helped direct public opinion toward the cause of the civil rights struggle and strengthened the resolve of civil rights workers to bring about a climate in the South that would not allow such violence against black children.

Then, in November 1963, the civil rights movement lost what its leaders considered one of its most powerful champions when President John F. Kennedy was assassinated. His Vice-

President, Lyndon B. Johnson, who was immediately sworn in as President, was from Texas, but he quickly put to rest any fears that he would backstep on civil rights. He promised to see through to completion the bills that Kennedy had hoped to see passed during his administration, and he would keep his promise. On July 2, 1964, he signed into law far-reaching civil rights legislation which contained new provisions to help guarantee blacks the right to vote, access to public accommodations such as hotels, motels, restaurants, and places of amusement, and authorized the federal government to sue to desegregate public facilities and schools, as well as many other important provisions aimed at ensuring that no citizen would be denied his or her rights because of race. Andrew Young helped to draft that bill.

In between coordinating campaigns like those in Birmingham, negotiating with white leaders, drafting SCLC position papers and working on the important Civil Rights Act of 1964, Young had continued in his role as director of the United Church of Christ voter registration drive. Having organized the basic structure and methods of encouraging people to register to vote and preparing them for eligibility, he had turned to the natural outgrowth of that basic program: training potential black officeholders. He realized that new black voters would not see much point in voting if they always had to choose among white candidates. Many of the local black leaders who later became sheriffs and mayors were graduates of the training programs Andrew Young developed.

By 1964 he had become so involved in and so valuable to the SCLC that he became executive director, and thereafter devoted all his time to the work of that organization. He went into the post in a year when his levelheaded approach to volatile situations was never more needed.

5 / Little Time to Be Afraid

The summer of 1964 was the most violent time of the civil rights era. The Student Nonviolent Coordinating Committee decided to conduct a huge voter registration drive in Mississippi and Alabama that summer, and hundreds of workers were arrested and jailed and beaten. John Lewis, then executive director of SNCC, was beaten up so many times in so many towns that he would later be unable to recall all the incidents. But the SNCC leaders and the student volunteers believed the only way they could show poor black farmers the importance of the vote was to risk their lives. The Congress of Racial Equality also planned an action in Mississippi that summer, a People-to-People March to dramatize the voter registration drive. On June 21, two young white CORE workers from the North and a black Mississippi civil rights worker who was acting as their guide disappeared near the town of

Philadelphia, Mississippi. In August their bodies were found in the mud of a dam built across the Tallahalla River near Philadelphia.

The SCLC started a campaign to desegregate public facilities in Saint Augustine, Florida, that summer, and there was terrible violence there as well. The Ku Klux Klan staged night marches and warned the demonstrators they would be stopped at all costs. But Andrew Young, who was in charge of the campaign, vowed their marches would continue. He personally led a march around the city's Old Slave Market, for it was the custom of the SCLC leaders to draw lots to determine who would lead what march, and the lot had fallen to Young for this one. The line was attacked, and Young was beaten to the ground by a blackjack-wielding white man. He lay there helpless. The other marchers had been programmed to stay in line, no matter what happened, but it was all they could do to keep from rushing to his rescue. They needed him at the negotiating table, not in the hospital. Fortunately, his injuries were not serious and he soon recovered, but after that it was decided within the SCLC that Andrew Young would henceforth leave a march or demonstration when it looked as if it might get violent. King told him he would not be of any help to the movement if he were beaten or jailed. Everyone had a job, and it was Young's job to stay healthy and out of jail so he would be able to negotiate with the white power structure.

"There were moments when you realized your lives were in danger," says Jean Young, "especially in the case of Andrew and the people who were constantly in the forefront of involvement. There were times when you did sober up and recognize the seriousness of it, but the majority of the time we just said to ourselves, 'This is the greatest thing that's ever happened in this country, and we're part of it, and it's wonderful.'

"We were all so very much involved. These people they

were writing about in the newspapers were the same people we'd had for supper the night before. We'd be sitting and talking with these students and other demonstrators who were being described in the papers [Southern white] as crazy radicals and agitators. There was so much activity, so much going on, and we were so intimately involved in all the stages of the Movement that there was very little time, really, to be afraid."

While her husband was in the forefront of the struggle, Jean Young played a quieter role. "I taught throughout the civil rights movement," she says, "and even though I was involved in all the major marches and demonstrations, I still had three children at home. I was the stable force in our family." She was always ready to open their home to groups of students on their way to and from one campaign or another, to stretch the meatloaf for unexpected supper guests, and to provide a supportive and peaceful atmosphere as her husband made decisions and developed campaigns that indirectly would have an effect on nearly all Americans.

Young was under a great deal of pressure then, as were the other leaders of the major civil rights organizations. As if it were not enough that they had to contend with the Ku Klux Klan and other racist whites, keep their workers in line and help them when they were beaten and arrested and jailed, they also had to be wary of one of their own country's most powerful agencies, the Federal Bureau of Investigation.

FBI agents followed civil rights leaders wherever they went. On the surface, this activity seemed natural, aimed at protecting the leaders, but it soon became apparent that the agents were also spying on them. Some very important people in the Kennedy Administration had hinted at what was going on back in 1963, but Young and the others knew it anyway. As he recalls, they could almost always expect to see a green Plymouth with a two-way radio in the parking lots of motels the SCLC people frequented. And when they saw one of those cars, they assumed that their rooms were bugged. "I'd usually walk around the motel . . . you look in the rooms, and the curtain is partially drawn, and you see a guy sitting down with earphones on and a tape recorder, and you know what he's listening to."

The bugging became a kind of joke with the SCLC people. Ralph Abernathy took to calling the bugs "doohickeys." "Did you hear that, doohickey?" he'd say. They christened the FBI tape recordings "golden records," and every time someone said something off-color or flip, King would laugh and warn, "Ol' Hoover's gonna have you in the Golden Record Club if you're not careful."

Given this situation, it is ironic that Martin Luther King, Jr., was chosen to receive the Nobel Prize for Peace that September of 1964. He was selected by the Norwegian Parliament above all other workers for peace in the world that year. The announcement caused great concern to white racists and probably to the FBI. King was scheduled to travel to Norway to receive the prize in December. Before his departure, a tape and an unsigned note were sent to him at SCLC headquarters. The note implied that he should commit suicide before the Nobel Prize awards or else disclosures would be made that would ruin his reputation.

King asked Young and a few other close advisers to listen to the tape with him. They listened but could not discern anything incriminating. The tape contained a casual conversation between King and a few other people followed by silence and then some sounds that indicated the performance of a sexual act, but those sounds could have been made by anyone at any time and in any place. Reporters were told that the FBI had evidence of wild parties and illicit sexual activities on the part of King and others in the SCLC, but none of the reporters was ever allowed to hear or see this FBI "evidence." The fact that FBI director J. Edgar Hoover was personally against

King soon became public knowledge. After King suggested that southern FBI agents were not as committed as they should be to investigating civil rights violations, Hoover called the 1964 Nobel Peace Prize winner "the most notorious liar in the country."

The last thing the SCLC leaders wanted was a feud with the director of the FBI, so they contacted his office and requested a meeting with Hoover. They met with him at FBI headquarters in Washington, D.C., on December 1, 1964, just a week before King was scheduled to leave for Oslo to accept the Nobel Prize. Young and the others had girded themselves for a hostile, argumentative Hoover, and they were caught completely off guard. The FBI director was full of praise for King and the SCLC. He congratulated King on winning the Nobel Prize and assured all the SCLC people that the FBI was doing everything it could in Mississippi to enforce the civil rights laws. In fact, he talked so much that the others rarely had a chance to get a word in. And when they did get a chance to speak, it didn't seem quite the time to bring up unpleasant matters. The Reverend Abernathy, who was the designated spokesman for the SCLC at the meeting, tried to find something nice to say about Hoover and the FBI. After the meeting ended, Cartha DeLoach, Hoover's assistant, and spokesmen for the SCLC held a press conference for an eager group of reporters who were sure the meeting had been an hour-long fight. When the reporters were told how friendly everyone had been, they refused to believe it.

Neither could King and Young and the others who had been present at the meeting. They felt as if they had been hoodwinked. Nothing substantial had even been discussed, let alone resolved. Perhaps, they reasoned, there had been too much publicity surrounding the meeting. King decided Young should set up an appointment to talk to Hoover alone, and Young did so.

Before meeting with Hoover, Young decided to gather some evidence. He met with members of the New York *Times* Washington Bureau and learned of the kinds of incriminating information FBI sources were giving to the *Times*: that King had a Swiss bank account and was taking for himself money earmarked for civil rights campaigns, that the SCLC had been infiltrated by communists, that movement leaders and members engaged in illicit sexual acts. Young hoped to get Hoover to explain how such slanderous and incorrect information could be coming from FBI sources without the knowledge of the director.

When Andrew Young arrived at FBI headquarters for his appointment with Hoover, he learned that he would not be meeting with the director after all but with DeLoach. Disappointed but determined to get some kind of explanation from the FBI about the false information that was being leaked to the press and to important church leaders, Young presented the information he had gathered. DeLoach assured him that the FBI would not do such a thing. Young told him he had personally caught FBI agents bugging the motel rooms of SCLC leaders, but DeLoach insisted that the FBI would not do something like that. Frustrated, Young left the meeting without having accomplished his purpose. He knew the FBI was engaging in illegal activity, but he could not get the agency to admit it. Many years later, after Hoover's death, the Senate Committee on Intelligence, looking into possible illegal activities on the part of the FBI, established that over a six-year period the FBI had made at least sixteen telephone taps on King's telephone and planted listening devices in at least eight of his hotel and motel rooms.

King's being awarded the Nobel Prize for Peace provided a big boost to the civil rights movement. It proved better than any other gesture that the rest of the world was keenly aware of the civil rights struggle in the U.S. South. People all over the world were pulling for him.

At thirty-five, King was the youngest man ever to be awarded the prize, but those close to him knew he was wise far beyond his years. They knew that his strong commitment to nonviolence was only one of the ways he displayed his commitment to peace. It took nearly as much energy and skill to keep peace within his own organization as it did to maintain a commitment to nonviolent methods in the civil rights struggle.

"There was always stress and strain within the SCLC, simply because there were so many dynamic individuals who were capable of doing such unique and creative things," says Jean Young. "Part of the brilliance of Martin Luther King was his capability of pulling together this kind of diverse group and making it work for a common cause. There was always a certain level of stress, but Martin, like a symphony conductor, managed to orchestrate the strengths of all of them.

"One of Andrew's strengths that Martin relied on was his sense of faith. He was an eternal optimist, and he would never allow things to get him down completely. He could always see the possibilities in the worst kinds of situations, and he was capable of some degree of humor because of his confidence that things were eventually going to work out."

Andrew recalls that King would use him to offset the urgings of more radical leaders in the SCLC. "He would try to use me to balance them out. He would expect me to take the conservative side, to sort of neutralize what [James] Bevel and Hosea [Williams] were trying to do, to give him an excuse to come down the middle. . . . He expected me to go 'way to the right [conservative side] on every question."

Sometimes the others would tease Young and call him the "Uncle Tom of the SCLC." They never said it with hostility. In fact, there was remarkably little hostility among the SCLC executive staff of fourteen, although there couldn't have been a more diverse group of personalities. They were all in the struggle together. Their methods differed, but their goals were the same. Their arguments at policy meetings were so heated and full of shouting that anyone who didn't know them would expect them to come to blows at any moment. Fifteen minutes after the meeting broke up, they could be giggling together like kids. There was genuine love among the SCLC leaders, a product of the experiences they had gone through together, the terrible danger, the arrests and white hostility, the victories they had won, and the basic respect they had for one another.

Sometimes Young adopted a conservative stance and sometimes he didn't. He tried to give good counsel, based on what he thought was right, and when leaders of the SCLC met to decide whether or not to participate in a massive voter registration drive SNCC was planning to begin in January 1965, in Alabama, he was in favor of participation. Selma, Alabama, where the drive was to begin, was a strongly segregated city, and insiders in the movement were predicting it could be another Birmingham. The SCLC hoped that by participating they could help keep the lines of communication to white authorities open, to keep the demonstrations and marches nonviolent.

The Selma campaign began in late January. After SNCC got things underway there, they moved on to Marion to help the people there organize their registration drive. Meanwhile, the SCLC had arrived in force in Alabama. They, too, were concentrating on Selma, but Young asked SCLC member Willie Bolden to go to Marion to represent the organization. Bolden spoke at an organizational meeting at a local church and after his speech an impromptu march to the Marion courthouse began. The marchers were met by state troopers, who began beating and arresting people. A young man named Jimmie Lee Jackson went to the aid of his mother, who was being beaten. Before he could get to her, he was cut down by bullets. Not much was made of the killing by the press, but many civil rights workers who were involved in the Alabama campaign believe that the murder of Jimmie Lee Jackson provided the impetus to much of the later campaign in Selma.

On February 1, 1965, King and Abernathy led about 800 people, most of whom were schoolchildren, in a march on the Selma courthouse. All were arrested and jailed. Marches held the next three days resulted in more arrests, some 3,000 in all, and Selma's jails were full to bursting.

On February 9 a federal court banned the literacy test and other technicalities that were used to deny registration to applicants, but the ruling had little effect on what was happening in Selma. The demonstrators kept marching and the police kept arresting until even the jails in neighboring towns were full. So Sheriff Jim Clark came up with a tactic other than arrest, the tactic of humiliation. On February 10 he and his deputies drove up in cars and trucks and surrounded a group of about 150 children who were demonstrating downtown. Then they drove the children out of town like cowboys herding cattle, forcing them to trot and prodding those who could not keep up, laughing at the children's discomfort. Television cameras were on the scene, and like the spectacle of children being attacked by fire hoses and police dogs in Birmingham, the sight of black children being treated like cattle disgusted viewers around the world. Young knew it was the right time to push for a negotiated settlement.

He had attempted to negotiate with white leaders of Selma earlier, but they had presented a united front in refusing his offers. Public Safety Director Wilson Baker, for example, had stood behind Sheriff Clark and the methods of dealing with the protesters that Clark had first proposed. In the meantime, Young had sized up the various leaders and identified those who might eventually be reasoned with and those who would

Martin Luther King, Jr., Ralph David Abernathy and Andrew Young lead a group of blacks to register to vote at the Selma courthouse during the voter registration drive that culminated in the Selma to Montgomery march.

(UPI)

never willingly compromise on segregation. He realized the reasonable men would be concerned about the blot on Selma's reputation and just as disgusted about the ill treatment of black children as other good people were. They would now be willing to negotiate. And so he again contacted Public Safety Director Baker. Baker was furious over Sheriff Clark's actions against the black children and refused to be allied with Clark any longer. Without Baker, the other white Selma leaders could no longer present a united front, and eventually the Selma campaign ended in victory for the civil rights movement.

In the meantime, the scenes of brutality in Selma and the murder of Jimmie Lee Jackson in Marion had caused many people who were sympathetic to the civil rights struggle to decide it was time to act. Hundreds of people, many from the North and many white, including a group of nuns from Chicago, converged on Selma. The campaign there was coming to an end, but SNCC especially did not want to waste the energy and commitment of these fresh supporters. SNCC decided that a march would be made from Selma to the state capitol in Montgomery, fifty-four miles away, where a delegation would try to meet with Alabama Governor George Wallace.

The SCLC, or at least the majority of its executive staff, was against the march, and on Sunday morning, March 7, a meeting was held at Brown's Chapel in Selma to determine whether or not the march would be held. Martin Luther King, Ralph Abernathy, and Andrew Young were back in Atlanta when Hosea Williams, who had remained in Selma, called to tell them about the meeting. King told Williams not to support the march. Young was so against it that he chartered a plane to Selma to try to talk SNCC out of it. But SNCC and its supporters would not back down. The world had to be told about Jimmie Lee Jackson and about the other brutalities in

Alabama. Hosea Williams informed the others in SCLC that the march would go on, with or without their support, so the SCLC leaders drew lots to determine who would be in the march. Hosea Williams was elected in this fashion.

That Sunday, March 7, 1965, came to be known as "Bloody Sunday." In the afternoon, several hundred people singing freedom songs started across the bridge over the Alabama River that led out of Selma toward Montgomery. At the other side, they were confronted by a line of state troopers on horseback. "This is an unlawful march," the troopers informed them. "You have three minutes to disperse." All the marchers knelt down where they were. Three minutes later, the troopers attacked. Some 150–200 pulled out gas masks and threw tear gas canisters, then went at the marchers with clubs. Many people ran screaming for cover, back across the bridge and along the streets of Selma to the safety of Brown's Chapel. And when the residents of the black community saw all those screaming, bloody people running for their lives, they got angry. And when they saw the troopers on horseback chasing the marchers, riding their horses up the steps of the churches in pursuit, they got furious. They ran to get their guns.

That frightened Andrew Young as much as the troopers with their horses and billy clubs and tear gas. It also frightened Wilson Baker, who was at the scene. Putting aside former animosities, he helped Young try to quiet the angry blacks. "He played such an important part of saving a bloodbath," Baker recalls. "He was just running wild up and down to these apartment units: 'Get back into the house with this weapon. . . . We're not going to have any weapons out.'" At length, Sheriff Jim Clark called off the troopers and peace was restored for a time.

A second attempt to march was also repulsed. Two days later, President Johnson sent federal troops to Alabama to protect the marchers. Once again, Andrew Young and others stepped in to negotiate. When the march that would succeed began, on March 21, only 300 marchers participated, by agreement, and by agreement, they were protected by hundreds of Army troops and National Guardsmen. But the presence of all those troops did not prevent the killing of Mrs. Viola Liuzzo. A white civil rights worker from Detroit, she was operating an automobile shuttle service for the marchers when she was shot to death on U.S. Highway 80 near Selma. She was shot March 25. The next day, President Johnson denounced the Ku Klux Klan and announced the arrest of four Klan members in connection with Mrs. Liuzzo's death. Four days later, the House Un-American Activities Committee voted to open a full investigation of the Klan and its "shocking crimes."

In Montgomery, an estimated 25,000 people awaited the marchers, who arrived in the capital safely. Governor Wallace twice refused to receive the delegation from the marchers, but finally he relented, again as a result of intense negotiation. The meeting took place on March 30. Yet another barrier against equal rights had fallen. Although it was primarily a symbolic victory, the fact that Governor Wallace, one of the most die-hard racists in public office in the South, had actually received a civil rights delegation was a victory for sure.

But more than symbolic victories were needed. Leaders of civil rights organizations had long realized that there should be a law specifically ensuring voting rights. Andrew Young had helped draft that kind of bill and had sent it to President Johnson. After Selma, Johnson too was convinced of the need for such a law. He took the draft Young had helped write, added his own comments, then presented it first to his staff and then to the Justice Department for reworking. When it was ready, he personally presented the bill to a joint session of Congress, ending his speech with the refrain that the civil rights movement had long used: "We shall overcome." The bill was passed, and on August 6, 1965, the Voting Rights Act

*After he won the Nobel Prize for Peace, Martin Luther King, Jr.,
was in great demand as a speaker all over the world. In 1965 he
was invited to give a sermon at the American Church in Paris,
France. Andrew Young accompanied him on that trip.*

(UPI)

was signed into law by the President. One of its most important provisions allowed black registrants who were turned
away by state officials to be registered by federal examiners.

The basic legal structure for guaranteeing equal rights to
black people had been laid, but the problems were far from
over. Racist southern whites would continue to resist integration, black voting, etc., but they would be disobeying the laws
of the land and liable to punishment for disobeying them.
Gradually most white southerners bowed to the inevitable,
and gradually black southerners began, by exercising their
newly won rights, to make a difference in the social and political structure in the South. In November 1965, Julian Bond,
former communications director of SNCC, became the first
black to be elected to the Georgia Legislature since the post-
Civil War Reconstruction period. The SCLC's Hosea Williams

would join him there in 1974. In 1965 more than 80 percent of Atlanta's registered black voters cast ballots in the Democratic primary. Among the white sheriffs who failed to win renomination was Selma sheriff Jim Clark. By July 1967 more than 50 percent of all eligible black voters in Mississippi, Georgia, Alabama, Louisiana, and South Carolina would be registered to vote.

The stage of action now shifted to the North, with whose blacks the civil rights leaders had not been much concerned, since they could vote, drink out of the same water fountains as whites, ride anywhere they wanted on public transportation, and eat in most of the same restaurants as whites. It had shocked not only the rest of the country but also many southern civil rights leaders when blacks in Watts, the black ghetto of Los Angeles, had rioted in the middle of August 1965. There had been riots in New York City, Rochester, New York, New Jersey, Philadelphia, and Chicago in 1964, but the Watts riot was much worse. Thirty-five people had been killed, twenty-eight of them blacks, nearly 900 injured, and millions of dollars' worth of property had been damaged. The riots in Watts reminded the southern civil rights leaders that there was a quieter segregation of blacks in the North. They might not live under segregated housing laws, but they were nevertheless confined to ghettos. Most could not afford to live elsewhere, and many of those who could found that the homes or apartments in white neighborhoods were "already rented" or that the banks were "unable" to give them home mortgages. Supposedly, there was no school segregation in the North, but because of housing patterns black children went to black schools and white children went to white schools. There was discrimination and segregation of all kinds in the North; it was simply more insidious, and much harder to fight.

Along with the realization within the SCLC that northern blacks had been almost entirely unaffected by the civil rights movement came the realization that if the nonviolent movement were not taken North, a violent movement would be. SNCC had been more militant than other civil rights groups from the beginning, but in 1966 it took a decidedly militant turn. New York-born Stokely Carmichael replaced John Lewis as executive director of SNCC in May 1966 and in June he openly voiced the new militancy, issuing a call for "Black Power!"

The leaders of the SCLC decided it was necessary, indeed essential, that the nonviolent crusade be taken North. It was needed by northern blacks nearly as much as it had been by southern blacks, and they needed to be shown that the nonviolent way was best.

Chicago was chosen as the first target city. The majority of black Chicagoans lived in substandard housing, worked at minimum-wage jobs, and were forced to send their children to segregated schools. In July 1966 the SCLC rented an apartment on the city's west side and on July 10 launched a drive to make Chicago an "open city." King and other members of SCLC began to take walks through the area, accompanied by the press, to point out housing violations and to talk about the kind of despair felt by people who lived in such neighborhoods. Two days later, blacks in the area began rioting. The riots lasted three nights, during which two blacks were killed, scores of policemen and civilians were injured, and more than 350 arrests were made. King met with Chicago mayor Richard Daley afterward and a four-point agreement to ease tensions in the city was announced. Tensions might have been eased between blacks and white authorities, but they were not eased between the SCLC and its supporters and racist whites. On August 5, as they led a march on Chicago's southwest side, King, Young, and other marchers were stoned by crowds of angry whites, who then did battle with the police who tried to stop them. The situation was just too volatile for the SCLC people and the very next day they left Chicago.

Still, the abortive campaign in Chicago made an impact and pointed up the unfairness of restricted housing. President Johnson expressed interest in the issue, and the SCLC submitted drafts of the kind of legislation that was needed. On February 15, 1967, Johnson proposed to Congress a new Civil Rights Act that contained, among other provisions, a special "open housing" clause. It would be the last time the SCLC and Johnson would agree on major issues. It would also be the last major civil rights legislation. More than a decade after the Montgomery bus boycott, a span of years that had seen thousands of demonstrations and protests and thousands more beatings and arrests (Hosea Williams was arrested some forty times), the civil rights workers could look back and realize they had wrought a major social revolution, a lasting one that would serve as a model for other social revolutions in this country, like the anti-war movement, the feminist movement, and the gay rights movement.

6 / End of an Era

Public interest had begun to shift from the civil rights movement to the anti-war movement by 1967. North Vietnam and South Vietnam in Southeast Asia were engaged in a civil war, and the United States had become increasingly involved in supporting South Vietnam, first with advisers, then with weapons, and now with troops. Many black people in the civil rights struggle felt that black leaders should stay away from the war issue, because it would dilute the energy of the black struggle. But other blacks felt that addressing the war issue was a logical extension of the campaign. After all, to provide troops to South Vietnam, the U.S. Army had to draft young men, and because fewer young black men than white were in college, or had connections in high places, more young black men were being sent to fight in Southeast Asia.

King had spoken out publicly against the escalating war in Vietnam in the spring of 1965. Adverse reaction had been so strong that he had refrained from making other public statements for a time. But the war had continued to escalate, and the very people who had supported or participated in the major civil rights battles had joined the anti-war movement. SNCC had taken a strong anti-war stand and former SNCC leader Julian Bond, elected to the Georgia Legislature in November 1965, had in January 1966 been denied his seat on the grounds that in opposing U.S. Vietnam policy he was guilty of disloyalty. It seemed to King, Andrew Young, and others in SCLC that they simply had to oppose American involvement in Vietnam no matter what the cost. Young felt particularly strongly that this action was a logical extension of the civil rights struggle, and that it was inevitable.

But the potential cost was high. Demanding that black people be guaranteed the same rights as their white fellow citizens enjoyed could not be viewed as un-American activity by anyone but members of the Ku Klux Klan or the ultra-conservative John Birch Society. Demanding that the United States cease all involvement in the war in Vietnam was another matter. Too many Americans saw the struggle as one between communism and democracy, and anti-war protesters as being anti-America and all that the country represented. Martin Luther King was not un-American and did not want to be charged with that offense, but when the United States began to drop bombs on North Vietnam he felt he could not remain silent.

The U.S. bombings flouted the charter of the United Nations. Thus, it was decided at SCLC that King would lead a mass anti-war demonstration at the U.N. in April 1967. There were all kinds of potential problems. Some elements of the anti-war movement were not just anti-U.S. involvement, but pro-North Vietnam. They liked to wave the flag of the Vietcong, the North Vietnamese guerilla fighters, and praise the leader of North Vietnam, Ho Chi Minh. They were highly vocal and could easily take over a demonstration whose purpose was not to support North Vietnam but to criticize U.S. involvement in the affairs of other nations. The SCLC realized they could lose control of the U.N. demonstration very easily if they were not careful, so Martin Luther King turned to Andrew Young, who had recently been named executive vice-president of the SCLC. He would be in charge of the demonstration, and one of his major duties would be to make sure the pro-North Vietnam people would not take command.

So Young started doing what he did best. Working quietly, behind the scenes, he made contact with the various factions of the anti-war movement. He did not insist that the more radical factions stay away, for he knew they would not. What he did was to negotiate with them about small but very important matters. The wavers of Vietcong flags could wave their flags, but they must keep their distance from Dr. King. Otherwise, it would appear that he supported them. Those who were in the habit of making anti-American statements must tone down their rhetoric. In return, Young reminded the radical factions of how much the appearance of Dr. King, the most respected black leader in the country and a Nobel Prize winner, would mean to the anti-war cause. The radical factions agreed to Young's terms, and the mass demonstration at the U.N. in April 1967 was a successful one. As Young had explained to the various factions that it must do, it appealed to the country's "better instincts."

Many other anti-war demonstrations did not, nor did many demonstrations by blacks at that time. The new militancy in the civil rights movement was probably a direct result of the years of nonviolent protest. Civil rights demonstrators had been able to take the brutality for just so long without fighting back, and when they felt they could no longer submit to white vio-

Despite the violence he had seen in Birmingham, Selma and else-where, Andrew Young remained committed to nonviolence. He explained this continued commitment and gave his definition of nonviolence at an SCLC convention in 1966.

(WIDE WORLD PHOTOS)

lence they turned against nearly all whites and against the philosophies of love and coequal existence. And then there were the many blacks who had never subscribed to any philosophy, who saw all the civil rights and anti-war protests and the violence that so often accompanied them, and just got caught up in it all and committed violence themselves, not against whites so much as against their own neighborhoods. During 1966 and 1967 there were major riots in Cleveland, Ohio; Jackson, Mississippi; Boston, Massachusetts; Tampa, Florida; Cincinnati, Ohio; Newark, New Jersey; Hartford, Connecticut; Philadelphia, Pennsylvania; Cambridge, Maryland; Milwaukee, Wisconsin; and many other cities. By July 1967, King and three other moderate black leaders, A. Philip Randolph, Roy Wilkins, and Whitney Young, felt the situation had gotten so out of hand that they issued a joint statement condemning and appealing for an end to the riots.

But the violence continued, and because it was not part of a movement at all, but a disorganized and destructive expression of anger and frustration, it could not be controlled even by the most militant black leaders. The SCLC did not attempt to step in, because trying to exercise any kind of control would have been dangerous and futile. Instead, the organization moved farther into the political arena. It had occurred to the SCLC leadership that the urban rioters had rioted not so much because they were black and discriminated against as because they were poor and discriminated against. They were ill-educated, poorly nourished and housed, medically neglected and underpaid, but as such they were no different from poor white people. The SCLC still had a purpose, its leaders decided, but it was a broader purpose, to bring to the attention of the federal government and the rest of the nation the plight of all poor people across the country. They would organize a Poor People's March on Washington to dramatize the plight of all the poor—black, white, red, brown, and yellow—in April of 1968.

Members of the SCLC executive staff began to crisscross the country, making speeches urging poor people to join the march. They also began to organize the march and plan for housing, feeding, and controlling all the marchers. As the time of the march approached, everyone was working at a frenzied pace. They really did not have time to go to Memphis, Tennessee, to support the cause of striking black sanitation workers there. But the Reverend Billy Kyles was a friend, and when he asked for help they could not refuse him. Besides, the striking workers had a reasonable grievance.

One Wednesday morning back at the end of January it had rained hard in Memphis. The sanitation men could not make their pickups, so the sanitation department called in the trucks after only two hours. That Friday, pay day, the black sanitation men found that while they had only been paid for two hours' work on Wednesday, the white workers had been paid for a full day's work. The black workers struck, demanding not just full pay for that rainy day but eight other considerations, including a fair system of promotion, back pay, sick pay, and vacation pay. Several days later the striking sanitation men staged a peaceful march on Main Street. Memphis police overreacted, beating the protesters and spraying a chemical irritant called Mace in their faces. The police action united the majority of the other black residents of Memphis behind the protesters, and soon the strike had mushroomed into a general protest against the entire racial situation in Memphis. Some segments of that black population were ready to meet violence with violence, and moderate leaders like the Reverend Kyles realized these people could easily take over if something were not done.

So the SCLC went to Memphis and Martin Luther King, Jr., accompanied by Bernard Lee, led a march on March 28. Suddenly he was pushed forward by a black teen-ager. Looking around him, he saw young blacks, many armed with sticks and "Black Power!" signs, converging on the marchers. The police were converging on the young militants. Lee decided this was no place to be and hustled King away to safety. The local newspapers charged that King had run away from the demonstration. Angry at this reaction, Young and others immediately drafted a statement to issue to the press denying that King had fled and stating that the troublemakers had been non-participants in the march.

King was very disturbed about the whole affair. He felt it was a blow to the nonviolent cause, a blow that could not be allowed to go unanswered. His advisers told him he should not blame himself. Young reminded him that violence was much too deeply rooted in American life for any individual or organization to take responsibility for it. Neither the SCLC nor King could reverse the trend. But King considered himself somehow responsible and felt it was his duty to show the world that the violent march had been an aberration.

Andrew Young remembers that his friend was very troubled, and that he had been for some time. "He couldn't relax. He couldn't sleep . . . other than the times that he spent with his family. Even when we were away on trips, he'd want to talk all night." Young was afraid that all the worry would affect King's health and that it would be cruelly ironic if he should be physically affected now, when the most dangerous days of the civil rights movement seemed to be behind them. "My feeling was that we had gotten past the Selmas and the dangerous days when we all took it for granted that we might die any day." Young urged King to get a physical examination and to start taking better care of himself.

Against the advice of his friends, King asked the leaders of the march to announce that he would lead a peaceful protest march through Memphis within the week. It was now up to others in the SCLC to make some fast plans. The SCLC had no strong organization in Memphis and thus could not take normal security precautions. Memphis police had offered protection to King, but he did not feel he could accept the offer without compromising his position as a preacher of nonviolence.

The march was scheduled for Monday, April 8. Hosea Williams and the Reverend Jesse Jackson, who had recently joined the SCLC, arrived in Memphis on Sunday, March 31, with others, and Andrew Young arrived on Monday, April 1. They thoroughly checked out the building and grounds of the Lorraine Motel, the black motel where they would be staying, made plans to station their own marshals along the route of the march, and decided never to leave King unguarded. Young set up a meeting between King and the Invaders, a militant gang suspected of having disrupted the first march, on April 3, the day King was to arrive in Memphis.

The plane that King and Abernathy took to Memphis on April 3 was delayed by a bomb threat, which did not ease the minds of any of his aides. But once he arrived in Memphis, things seemed to go well. The meeting with the Invaders went smoothly, and King managed to get their assurance that they would not disrupt the coming march. That evening, he spoke extemporaneously at a meeting at the Mason Street Temple. Because he had not expected to speak, he had no written remarks prepared, so he simply began talking, and at length he turned to the subject of his own safety. He spoke about how he would like to be remembered after he died. He spoke movingly and passionately, and when he had finished the crowd leaped to their feet, cheering. But those who were close to him were not excited by his speech. They knew that he had never before spoken with such deep feeling about himself in public.

"We never really talked about death," says Andrew Young. "It just never came up except once or twice, in a joking sort of way. I remember one night, during a Mississippi visit, Martin and I were driving to Natchez although officials had just warned us of an assassination threat. About an hour out of

Jackson, this strange-looking car slowed down in front of us. It just sat there awhile. Martin said jokingly, 'Lord, they gonna blow us right off of this highway!' Fortunately, I was the one who was sitting at the wheel. I stepped on the gas and passed that car at ninety miles an hour."

It was different here in Memphis, and King's aides were worried. They knew that the city was like a powder keg waiting to explode. The Ku Klux Klan had warned of a retaliatory march. The White Citizens Council had been holding an emergency membership drive. Hate literature had been distributed all over the city. As Young accompanied King out a side door after the meeting at the Temple, he realized King knew it, too.

Young wanted to stay with his friend, but his work was not yet over. He was scheduled to attend a strategy meeting with strike leaders at 11 p.m. After that, he and King were to go to the home of Judge Ben Hooks, a black leader in Memphis. They drove to the Minimum Salary Building. Young went upstairs to meet with the union people, after making sure that the union's community relations representative would be outside to keep an eye on King. Young left the meeting as soon as he could and returned to the car. King asked him how the meeting had gone and he gave a brief report. Young did not ask what King had been thinking about, sitting there alone in the car. He started the engine and drove to the home of Judge Hooks. They did not return to the Lorraine Motel until after 3 a.m.

Thursday, April 4, was filled with meetings and strategy sessions, for the march was only four days away and there was still much to do. Andrew Young spent most of the day in federal court representing King at the hearing on the injunction against further marching that had been handed down a few days earlier. Assuming that the others would not expect him until they saw him, he did not bother to call the motel during recesses in the hearing. When the court adjourned late in the afternoon, he returned to the motel and made his way to room 306, where King was sure to be.

He was, as were Abernathy, King's younger brother A.D., Hosea Williams, Bernard Lee, James Bevel and others. As Andrew Young appeared in the doorway, Abernathy called out in mock surprise, "Well, look who's here!" And before Young could react he had been caught in a bear hug and wrestled to the floor. Five grown men were on top of him, pinning him down. They let him up just enough to see King, his finger raised in a scolding gesture. "You think you can always go off on your own?" King demanded. "How many times must we tell you, you got to call in, man!"

King continued, "You know, Ralph and I were going to call you in court, pull you right out of that room and bawl you out. Now we're going teach you a lesson!" They tickled him unmercifully and when he was weak from laughter they started wrestling with each other until they were all exhausted. Panting from laughing so hard, Young raised himself up off the floor and settled into a chair. He looked around at his friends and realized how worried about him they had been, off by himself in a hostile town, and how great was the tension they all felt. Thank God they were so close that they could release that tension by tickling and wrestling with each other.

That evening they had all been invited to dinner at the home of the Reverend Billy Kyles and after that there was another mass meeting to attend at the Mason Street Temple. Young had showered and dressed by 5:30. He went down to the parking lot and joined the others waiting there—King's attorney Chauncey Eskridge, Hosea Williams, James Bevel, Jesse Jackson, and Kyles. They talked quietly and from time to time looked up to the balcony hoping to catch some glimpse of King and Abernathy, who were still getting dressed. At length, Kyles went up the stairs to see what was taking so long. Just then, King appeared on the balcony to shout a few last-minute instructions to his aides. He then turned to re-enter the room. "Oh, Doc—" Jackson began, and King turned back toward the balcony. Suddenly there was a shotgun blast. Young crouched down, then stood straight up and looked up at the balcony. With the others, he raced to the place where King had been standing and found him lying in a pool of blood. Young knelt to feel his friend's pulse. Feeling something, he shouted for help.

In the horror and confusion, Kyles managed to call an ambulance and Young and the others managed to point to the direction from which the shot seemed to have come. Hundreds of helmeted police had suddenly materialized. An ambulance was on its way, but somehow Young knew King would not live. He remembered how King had worried about whether or not he was doing the right thing and intimated that his life might be taken. But somehow, Young had not thought that King would go alone. He had thought they would all go together, victims of some sort of mass assassination or a bomb back in Selma or Birmingham or Montgomery.

When the ambulance arrived, they all went to St. Jude's Hospital. Andrew Young went to a pay telephone outside the emergency room to call Coretta King in Atlanta. She had already been notified of the shooting and was dressing for the flight to Memphis, but Young realized how important it would be to her to see her husband before he died. Martin was in critical condition, he told her, but he was *not* dead. Then he returned to the waiting room and sat there with his head in his hands as doctors worked feverishly over Martin Luther King. But they could do nothing. At length, Abernathy emerged from the emergency room to tell them that King was gone, and Young realized that Ralph needed him. With Chauncey Eskridge, he helped Abernathy out the door to face the reporters and television cameras.

Andrew Young had a funny feeling about his friend's death. After they had returned from the hospital, he took Abernathy aside and asked him if Martin had confided anything to him about FBI harassment or any threats on his life. Abernathy told him King had said nothing, but that did not allay Young's suspicions. "We were confronted by a black community that was losing faith in nonviolence, saying nonviolence couldn't deal with the economic problems, nonviolence wouldn't work in the North. And our answer was, well, maybe the kind of marches that we had in the South would not work, but that massive civil disobedience would work. And so we had escalated the rhetoric of nonviolence—not Martin himself, but me and Bevel and Hosea and everybody else—so that there was a real fear of Martin coming to Washington with thousands of people to disrupt the life of the government. And some of the kinds of things that were in the newspapers and in the Congressional Record around that time lead me to think that there would have been people in the federal government somewhere that made a decision that Martin had to be stopped."

Subsequently James Earl Ray, an escaped convict, was captured and convicted of shooting King. Ray insisted that he had merely been a paid gunman but he refused to identify any co-conspirators. Some observers felt Ray was lying, that he had acted alone. But others, including Andrew Young, felt that Ray had been helped. When the Senate Intelligence Committee investigated the FBI and found that the agency had indeed spied on King illegally, that reinforced the feelings of those who believed the FBI might have been involved in King's assassination. Continuing doubts about both the assassination of King and that of President Kennedy led another Senate committee to reopen the investigations of both murders to try to determine once and for all if either was the result of a conspiracy. At this writing, nothing had been proven conclusively.

Andrew Young and the others had no time to be alone with

their grief. They had to regroup, quickly. An emergency meeting was held at the Lorraine Motel that night. King had said that if anything should happen to him, he wanted Abernathy to succeed him; remembering that, all of them were willing to look to Abernathy as their leader. They decided to go on with the Poor People's March on Washington. They made tentative plans for funeral services, agreeing that Coretta King would make the final decisions. They telephoned the Memphis police and requested protection for Abernathy. They went to bed for the few hours that remained of the night, wondering why it had happened in Memphis, wondering why it had happened to *him* alone.

The assassination of Martin Luther King, Jr., signaled the

Andrew Young attends a memorial service commemorating Martin Luther King, Jr.'s, 47th birthday. Even eight years after his friend's death, Young could still be moved to tears when he thought about how much he, and the world, had lost.

(UPI)

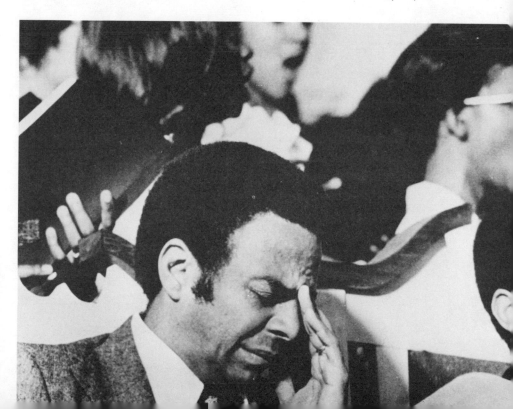

end of the civil rights movement, although it had been on the way out, really, since about 1966. Andrew Young was only one of many who mourned not just the death of his friend but the end of the movement. "It was probably the happiest time of my life. It was rough, but the issues were very clear-cut. We knew what we had to do and we had a group of people pretty much committed to doing it."

7 / Why Not Run
for Congress?

Jean Young recalls, "After Martin's death, many of the people involved closely with the movement underwent some really intense soul-searching—where do we go from here and what happens to the movement and what is my role in the movement?—and certainly this was something Andrew had to do. He felt very strongly that Ralph Abernathy should be the head of the Southern Christian Leadership Conference. At that time this was the most natural thing in the world, and so there were no yearnings on his part to take that leadership role. Under such circumstances there are always people who think there should be a change, and there was a group that was trying to promote different people. But he never had any interest in doing it. He wasn't sure what he should do. It was a time of great introspection for Andrew."

After King's death, Ralph David Abernathy and Andrew Young explain at a press conference that henceforth the SCLC would pursue a more conservative strategy that stressed voter registration and political action campaigns.

They all still needed to act, however, and the first order of business was the Poor People's Campaign that had been in the planning before King's death. The SCLC announced that it would still be held, and the tremendous influx of funds and volunteers that came as a result of King's death made it possible. Some 3,000 people participated in the two-month-long campaign, which began May 11. Resurrection City, U.S.A., was built near the Lincoln Memorial. A canvas-and-plywood encampment, it housed all who came, and had been arranged for with the police. But when the SCLC's demonstration permit expired June 24, the police closed Resurrection City. No significant legislation resulted from the campaign.

While the Poor People's Campaign was in progress, Robert Kennedy was slain in Los Angeles. The brother of the slain President was himself campaigning for the Democratic presidential nomination at the time, for Lyndon B. Johnson had announced that he would not run for office again. Andrew Young supported Kennedy's bid for the nomination. Kennedy had attended King's funeral, which had touched Young. He had spoken with the former attorney general who was now a senator, and come to believe that Robert Kennedy felt much the same as his slain brother had about black people's and poor people's rights. Thus, the assassination was a blow to Young. "I was so busy keeping the movement going after Martin's death that I never stopped to feel it till Bobby died," he says. "Then it all came down."

The deaths of King and Kennedy, the anti-war movement, the trend to militancy within the civil rights struggle—all these factors had combined to bring about the end of an era, and the end of the real power of the SCLC. Young realized that the SCLC was no longer strong enough to take an important stand on national issues. In the middle of 1969, with Abernathy and the others he mapped out a new strategy, a more conservative one that stressed voter registration and political action campaigns. Before the new strategy was begun, however, the SCLC was called upon one more time to help out in what seemed like a stalemate situation.

In 1969, low-paid black workers in the medical college at Charleston, South Carolina, went out on strike against the college. The president of the institution, Dr. William McCord, refused to grant any of the workers' demands. In fact, he refused even to negotiate. The workers, in turn, refused to end the strike. By early 1970 the situation was at such an impasse that the strikers appealed to the SCLC for help, and as the organization's chief negotiator, Andrew Young went to Charleston. He contacted McCord, who agreed to meet with him. In

the interim, Young did some checking. He learned that Mc-
Cord's father had been a missionary, and that interested him.
After all, he had once wanted to be a missionary. According to
Charleston congressman Mendel Davis, that mutual tie was all
that Andrew Young needed: "Andy got the conversation started
on that basis—not as a black talking to a white but as a man of
the cloth talking to a guy whose father had been the same
thing." It did not take long at all for Young to negotiate an
agreement that ended the strike, and not a few people in
Charleston developed admiration, if not downright awe, for
Andrew Young.

Young realized that the next important arena for black people was the political one. Black people had secured the right
to vote. Now it was time to use their votes to bring about
needed changes in the South. "There just comes a time when
any social movement has to come off the street and enter politics," he contends. "India's example is a case in point: the
National Congress Party which inherited independence was an
extension of Gandhi . . . and the case is repeated for prac-
tically every successful movement." But the notion of running
for political office himself apparently did not occur to Andrew
Young until late 1969 or early 1970.

Nineteen-seventy was an election year, and the veteran freedom fighters felt it was time that a black ran for Congress from
the South. Georgia's Fifth Congressional District, which included most of Atlanta, was at that time represented by
Fletcher Thompson, a conservative who rarely bothered to visit
the black neighborhoods in the district. A strong black candidate just might be able to unseat Thompson. The problem was
to find that strong black candidate.

Jean Young recalls, "John Lewis was trying to get Julian
[Bond, who had been elected to the Georgia Legislature in
1965 and had eventually been allowed to take his seat] to run

for Congress. He wrote a letter to Julian in which he enumer-
ated all the reasons why he thought Julian would be a good
candidate. But Julian, for reasons of his own, decided he was
not interested in doing that. And so Andrew and John were
talking about it on a plane somewhere, and Andrew saw the
letter and all of a sudden he began to realize that all the char-
acteristics John Lewis had listed in regard to Julian Bond—his
ability to raise funds outside Atlanta, his ability to draw a cross-
section of people, etc.—almost all the criteria John Lewis
thought important for a candidate applied to him also. This was
really the spark of the idea.

"The next thing I knew he was calling me on the telephone
and saying, 'What do you think about running for Congress?'
It was completely out of the blue! Never before in *any* of our
long, all-night talk sessions had he ever mentioned running for
political office."

Jean Young was willing to try. Neither she nor her husband
was particularly concerned about the fact that no black congressman had been elected from the south in nearly a century.
The civil rights movement had taught them that things that
"couldn't be done" could be done anyway. But both she and
Andrew realized that deciding to try was just the first step.
A political campaign required both money and manpower, and
a lot of each. The money question was partially answered when
Young went to New York. "He began to throw the idea around
with some friends like Harry and Julie Belafonte and Stoney
Cooks, brother of Julie Belafonte, and they just took the idea
and ran," Jean recalls. "They all were so excited about it, and
they decided to have a fund-raiser."

There were plenty of blacks in Atlanta who were willing to
contribute funds to the campaign, and Jean Young found her-
self in charge of throwing quite a few fund-raising parties her-
self.

Manpower turned out to be no problem either. With the

support of Abernathy, Coretta Scott King, Julian Bond, John Lewis and many others, Andrew Young put together a strong political organization of hardworking volunteers, both black and white, many of them veterans of the civil rights struggle. Stoney Cooks, who had left Anderson College in Anderson, Indiana, to join the Selma to Montgomery march and then joined the SCLC staff, proved a particularly valuable organizer. Assured of both financial support and personnel, Andrew Young entered the Democratic primary race in the spring of 1970. His opponents in the primary election would be two whites and another black, Lonnie King. King had participated in the first sit-ins in Atlanta with Julian Bond in the early 1960s when both were students at Morehouse College. Both had later joined the Student Nonviolent Coordinating Committee. Lonnie King's credentials as a civil rights activist were thus impressive, and some blacks in Atlanta feared that the two would split the black vote and enable one of the white candidates to win the primary, but it was King who was considered the potential spoiler. The majority of black leaders supported Andrew Young as the more levelheaded and less militant and thus as the more effective of the two men.

Black leaders and black voters, however, were not going to decide either the primary election in September or the general election in November, for the district in which they were running was predominantly white. Georgia's Fifth Congressional District was only 29 percent black, and for any black candidate to win, he would need some of the 71 percent white vote.

The primary election campaign was a difficult one for Andrew Young. He disliked having to run against Lonnie King. He also disliked running a campaign based on personalities rather than issues, but King's supporters emphasized personalities, or more accurately, styles. They pointed out that King had been on the front lines of the movement, while Young had played a more behind-the-scenes role. The implication was that King would be more likely to be out on the front lines fighting for his constituents; but the voters did not buy it. In the primary election, Young received 34,330 votes to King's 7,997. But as had been feared, the presence of two black candidates had split the black vote. Young's vote total was not high enough to assure him a clear victory. A white candidate named Lowe had won 21,586 votes, forcing a run-off election between himself and Young. Andrew Young won that election with a clear victory, capturing 59.8 percent of the vote to Lowe's 40.2 percent. There was a happy celebration in the Young home that night, but everyone knew the big victory remained to be won. In two months, Andrew would face Fletcher Thompson in the general election.

Jean Young was very active in the campaign, not just hosting fund-raising parties and feeding scores of volunteers, but speaking before church groups and civic organizations and in shopping centers and parking lots. "It was the most exciting campaign of all," she recalls, "because no one believed it was possible for a black to be elected to Congress in the South at that time."

No one, that is, except Andrew Young. His optimism was boundless, but it stemmed from faith more than from a realistic view of the facts. "If a white majority elects a black man to Congress, it will say that the American dream is still possible and it will restore faith in this country and in the political process for a lot of people—the young and the poor and the black—those groups that are most alienated," he told a New York *Times* reporter in the summer of 1970.

There were white southerners who shared this view. "Sometimes," says Jean Young, "we got support from very unexpected sources. Lillian Carter was one. At the time, Jimmy Carter was campaigning for governor. Andrew and I were out campaigning and Miss Lillian, as they call her, had come to one of the meetings representing her son's candidacy. We met her and she was very taken with Andrew, and he with her, and that was our introduction to the Carter family."

During that meeting with Lillian Carter, Andrew Young talked with her at length and learned about her experiences in the Peace Corps and in India. He "fell in love" with the courageous elderly woman, who made a financial contribution to his campaign. But he was suspicious of her son. When Carter visited Pascal's restaurant, a meeting place for black politicians in Atlanta, Young was impressed by the way the candidate shook hands and talked with the kitchen staff with as much care as he did the politicians in the restaurant. "I realized there was something really genuine and solid about this guy," he later recalled, "but I was still scared to vote for him. I had the notion that nothing good could come from South Georgia, especially Plains. It was still hard to believe in a southern white politician." In the Democratic primary, Young voted for Carl Sanders, the incumbent governor, but after Carter won the primary Young supported him against his Republican opponent.

The Carters were the exception rather than the rule in the South at that time. Many white southerners believed the South would be destroyed if blacks were elected to high office. The bitter primary fight with Lonnie King had not helped Andrew Young in this regard, for it had created unpleasant images of black in-fighting in the minds of white voters. Young admits that his campaign strategy only made matters worse. "Let's face it, there is still a hard-core element of racists in the South. But there is also a growing new liberal white vote. In Atlanta, we like to call it our New South Coalition: black votes, liberal votes, white labor votes. Now the problem is to involve those new white voters without stirring up the dyed-in-the-wool racists in the process. It's difficult. In 1970 we sent white volunteers into certain white areas. It didn't work. Many of the whites were as resentful of those kids as they would have been of black people banging on their doors."

It also didn't help the Young campaign that white Republican opponent Fletcher Thompson appeared to run his own campaign based primarily on the warning that a victory for Young would signal the end of Western civilization. The film clips that Thompson ran as part of his campaign were designed to frighten white voters, particularly those in southern Fulton County suburbs where middle-class whites were extremely uneasy about the black ghetto next door in Atlanta. In the general election Thompson beat Young 78,486 to 58,720 votes.

Having beaten Young in 1970, Thompson is in a position to be charitable. Nevertheless, his opinion of Young is similar to most other people's in Atlanta. "Andy Young was the most honorable of all my opponents," he said in 1976. "We just don't see eye to eye on fiscal matters or on political philosophy. I am a conservative and he is a liberal."

Despite his former optimism, Andrew Young was forced to conclude that the South was not yet ready for a black congressman. Still, he was not ready to give up. Congressional elections would come up again in two more years.

Having resigned from his post as executive vice-president of the SCLC to run for Congress, Young found himself momentarily without a job. But soon he accepted a post as chairman of the Atlanta Community Relations Commission and plunged into work for the city that had denied him the job he had really wanted. Jean Young, meanwhile, had become a curriculum research specialist with the Atlanta public schools and was busily engaged in helping to found Atlanta Junior College. Despite their busy schedules, the period between 1970 and 1972 was the most relaxed they had enjoyed in years. For the first time in a decade, Andrew Young had a fairly regular schedule.

Part of his job was to boost Atlanta—to talk about its good points, to encourage businesses to locate there, to solve disputes among its citizens. Thus, when a British Broadcasting

Corporation reporter came to Atlanta a few months after Jimmy Carter was elected governor to do a story on Carter, Andrew Young was a natural person for him to contact for comment. Quoting part of Carter's inaugural address, "No poor, rural, weak or black person should ever have to bear the additional burden of being deprived of the opportunity of an education, a job, or simple justice," the reporter said he thought it was remarkable that a white southerner could speak such words. Young thought it less remarkable than practical, based on a realistic awareness of growing black voting power. Carter was "ideologically ignorant," said Young, but from time to time he did the right thing.

Andrew Young's remarks got back to Carter and, afraid that the governor would misunderstand them, Young called him to explain what he really meant. Rather than finding an angry Carter, Young found himself being invited to a reception at the governor's mansion. He was growing to like Carter, despite his misgivings.

A few months after the 1970 election, the Legal Defense Fund of the National Association for the Advancement of Colored People went to court to protest the alignment of the Fifth Congressional District in Georgia. Recently released federal census figures showed that the proportion of blacks had increased over the preceding ten years, and the NAACP felt that the district lines should be redrawn to reflect the city's population better. The suit was successful. The new Fifth Congressional District included the greater part of metropolitan Atlanta plus a rural area just north of the city. It also included the majority of Atlanta's black voters, but there were still many white neighborhoods—in fact, white voters were still in the majority, with 62 percent. Young realized that he would be facing much the same problems in this campaign as he had in 1970 if he ran for Congress again. Still, he decided to run.

Early in 1972, he resigned from the Atlanta Community Relations Committee and announced his candidacy for the congressional seat. This time he faced little opposition in the Democratic primary, but his Republican opponent in the general election would not be Fletcher Thompson. Court-ordered redistricting had removed south Fulton County, Thompson's most solid base of support, from the Fifth Congressional District, so Thompson had decided to run for the Senate—unsuccessfully, as it turned out. The chief Republican contender for Thompson's old congressional seat was Rodney M. Cook, and he was very different from Thompson. Cook had worked in the civil rights struggle in the 1950s and 1960s; he was a moderate in political matters. Young had expected to be running against a segregationist and he had not looked forward to Thompson's racist tactics. With Cook as his opponent, he looked forward to a campaign based on issues rather than on race.

With most of the black votes in the district assured, Young concentrated on the white voters, but having learned from his experience in the 1970 campaign he did it in a more low-keyed manner. He spent much time in the white neighborhoods, opposing construction of freeways that would reduce property values, promising to clean up the polluted Chattahoochee River. Miss Lillian Carter again contributed to his campaign, and so did Jimmy Carter's son, Chip. Jimmy Carter invited Andrew Young over to the governor's mansion a few times and also telephoned him periodically. Young never minced words when he expressed his views to Carter and was surprised to learn that Carter often agreed with him. Carter believed that Young would win the election and wanted the black leader on his side. Nineteen seventy-two was also a presidential election year, and at the Democratic Nominating Convention in June, where South Dakota Senator George McGovern was nominated as the party's presidential candidate, Young, at Carter's request, suggested Carter to McGovern as a possible running mate. He, in turn, wanted the governor on his side. McGovern would choose another running mate, and in November 1972 Republican Richard Nixon would be re-elected as President, but the first, tentative political relationship between Andrew Young and Jimmy Carter was established at the time.

The 1972 congressional campaign between Andrew Young and Rodney Cook was devoid of racial issues except for one, and it was a major one. Although opponents of court-ordered school busing generally insist that the issue is one of individuals' rights, it usually becomes at least partly a racial issue, for it involves busing black children and white children to achieve racial integration. Young was in favor of busing; Rodney Cook was against it, and so were many whites in the Fifth Congressional District. A few weeks before the election, a federal court ordered the Atlanta school system to institute busing to bring about integration. Many of Young's supporters believed the unpopular decision would cost him votes, but he refused to be drawn into a single-issue campaign. He ran on a progressive platform with slogans like "Think Young" and "Young Ideas for Atlanta." Cook later accused him of having run a "black campaign" and of being more concerned with fame and fortune than with the people of the district.

Election day in November 1972 was rainy and cold. Such weather usually promised a low voter turn-out, but that political adage did not apply on that day. A large percentage of citizens voted, and when the ballots were counted Andrew Young had won, 72,289 to 64,495. His total was 53 percent of the vote, including almost all the black votes and nearly one quarter of the white votes. What was even more encouraging was that Young's victory had not been on the coattails of the Democratic presidential candidate, for whom the voters had cast their ballots on the same day. Often, voters will make their choice for President, then vote for all the candidates in the

In 1972, Andrew Young became the first black congressman to be
elected from the South since Reconstruction.

same party, right down the line. But in Georgia's Fifth Congressional District the voters chose Republican Richard Nixon over Democrat George McGovern by almost the same percentage as they chose Democrat Andrew Young over Republican Rodney Cook.

That night, a few well-meaning friends hired a group of security guards to protect Andrew Young and his family, for they feared white backlash over his victory. Although the Youngs appreciated the gesture, they couldn't help laughing about it. If they'd managed to get through the civil rights struggle unharmed, they were not very worried about safety now. There was a truly joyous celebration at Andrew's headquarters that night, for he had done it! He had become the first black to be elected to Congress since Reconstruction. He was also one of the first two blacks to be elected from the entire South since the turn of the century. Over in Texas, a lawyer named Barbara Jordan shared that happy distinction with him.

Andrew Young now faced a new challenge. He would have to prove that he meant his campaign promise to address issues, not race. He knew that many of Atlanta's white business leaders distrusted him. He'd been so close to Martin Luther King, Jr., and so deeply involved in the civil rights struggle that they believed he was a revolutionary who would not represent Atlanta's whites in Washington. What he wanted to do was to gain the respect of those businessmen and his other white constituents while helping his black constituents.

"I've never been given to a lot of blacker-than-thou rhetoric and that will not be the style that I'll adopt in Washington," he explained to the reporters who besieged him after the election. "I think we have to find ways to escape what we now recognize was an essentially paternalistic approach to the problems of the black community. We have to find the kinds of programs that deal with the structural issues of poverty and unemployment by linking together the needs of black people and the needs of the rest of society. A rapid transit system, for example, which everyone needs, can actually create more employment than some special training program for jobs that ultimately turn out not to exist. I think this is the direction in which we must head."

8 / A Man of "Sweet Reason"

The 93rd Congress convened on January 3, 1973. Along with other new legislators, including Congresswoman Barbara Jordan of Texas, Andrew Young took the oath of office from Speaker of the House Carl Albert. After the brief session, he went to his office in the Cannon House Office Building, where friends and family gave a small party for him. By his side was Stoney Cooks, his friend and supporter, whom he had chosen as his chief aide. Neither one was familiar with Washington, D.C., and the way things were done in Congress, but both were confident they would learn quickly. One thing they learned very quickly was that being a freshman in Congress was rather like being a freshman in high school or college. There were so many rules, so much red tape, so much protocol, and even if a freshman did his homework it did not do him much good. There was a kind of unspoken rule in the House that freshmen were to be seen and not heard.

Having no seniority, Young had little choice in committee assignments. He was placed on the House Banking and Currency Committee, when he would have preferred to serve on a committee that had more direct involvement with the problems of poor people. He had all kinds of ideas for new legislation, but he soon learned that getting a bill passed was a very complex process. One of the first things he learned was that all the other 400-odd representatives also had all kinds of ideas for new legislation, or at least for new bills. Because they came up for re-election every two years, they were impelled to *produce*, even if their production was just words on paper. Quantity seemed to count more than quality, and there was a constant scramble by the representatives to go on record as having introduced X-number of bills per term. They seemed to feel that their constituents would be properly impressed and would not notice how few of the bills that had been introduced had actually been passed.

The nature of the legislative process was such that all these introduced bills could really clog the Congress. For a bill to pass in the House, for example, it must first be introduced on the floor of the House. It then goes to the appropriate committee for study. Once that committee has considered that bill—and it may not get around to considering it for a long time—it may "table" the bill, or put it away for later consideration. Many bills never get out of committee. For a bill to be considered by the House, it must be voted out of committee. When a bill does come before the House for consideration, amendments to it are usually introduced, and each must be voted on. If the Senate has a similar bill pending, a joint committee may be assigned to come up with a unified bill. The amended bill, or unified bill, must then be passed by a majority of both houses of Congress. If the bill does pass, it goes to the

President for signing. He may sign it, veto it, or "pocket-veto" it by doing nothing. Either kind of veto must then be over-ridden by a two-thirds majority of both the House and the Senate before it can become law. This whole process is part of the checks-and-balances system that is essential to a real democracy, but it is probably safe to assume that our coun-try's founding fathers could not foresee what kind of legislative mess the Congress could get into two hundred years later, with hundreds of congresspeople introducing bills ranging from major legislation affecting all Americans to bills declaring, say, October 1 as National Hot Dog Day, or earmarking federal funds to clear out the litter in the Okefenokee Swamp, nearly all of which had, as stipulated by the Constitution, to go through the same legislative channels. Understandably, it seemed to many eager new members of Congress that the channels most in need of anti-pollution action were those in the government.

Having learned all these facts of Washington life, Andrew Young never regretted for a moment having sought a seat in Congress. "He enjoyed the platform he had to get across ideas," says Jean Young. "It was a very broad platform. Speaking for the basic needs of people was what he felt strongly about, and he felt this was a real opportunity for him to let others know about the needs of just ordinary people."

Realizing he could make the most effective use of that platform if he used it properly, he devoted himself to learn-ing all he could about the workings of Congress in addition to performing his duties as a congressman. Those duties were several. Besides serving on the Banking and Currency Com-mittee, he also was a member of the Congressional Black Caucus, and nearly every weekend while Congress was in ses-sion he returned home to Atlanta.

A major reason for returning home was to see his family and particularly his and Jean's brand-new child, Andrew Jack-

son Young, III, who came to be called Bo almost immediately.
"Bo was born right after Andrew was sworn into Congress,"
says Jean Young. "He was sworn in in January and Bo was
born in February. I never really stopped working because
of his birth. I was still teaching, and with Andrew in Washington so much it was important for him to spend time with
his son. And it was important for me to have some time *away*
from him! So Andrew would take Bo to Congress with him,
and he'd sleep on a little rug under Andrew's desk. He was
always very much around, in Congress, in all the campaigns,
and everywhere we've gone, so he's a very political child."

Young also returned so frequently to Atlanta because he
realized it was important for him to maintain close contact
with his constituents. "I'm going to be a *working* representative," he said shortly after his election. "That's how we won—
we got out and worked. I try to tell these young people: it's not
always the good guy who wins the election, but the man who
works harder. If the better man just happens to work a little
harder, then he wins, but bad guys are usually up early in the
morning. I intend to visit my district every weekend. Church
on Sunday, a school every Monday. That's doubly important
where black people are concerned. We're terribly cynical
about people we don't see. We don't read too much about our
men in the paper, so it's their physical presence and acces-
sibility that counts."

So he made himself accessible to his constituents, and on
the floor of Congress he voted for or against measures depend-
ing on how those measures would affect them. Among the
measures he consistently voted against during his first term in
Congress were budget cuts proposed by the Nixon Administration that would affect money for health, welfare, housing, urban
development, sewage treatment plants, and community development. As he wrote in an article for *The Nation* in May 1973,
"The proposed fiscal 1974 budget is obviously the most anti-

people budget in modern history. It is clearly not anti-inflationary and it is clearly not equitable. The blacks, the poor and the aged have few advocates within the Administration or in the agencies created to administer the overall economic policies." He also voted to override the President's veto of the War Powers Bill limiting Executive war-making powers, and against military aid to South Vietnam.

One of his first acts as a congressman was to introduce legislation prohibiting the transfer of NATO equipment to Portuguese military factions in Angola, Mozambique, and Guinea-Bissau, all former Portuguese colonies. He voted for court-ordered busing to achieve integration and for government aid to poor women who wanted abortions. He voted against appropriating monies for a new B-1 bomber, anti-ballistic missiles, and nerve gas.

He supported a bill that would allow Americans to register to vote by mailing in postcards and took the opportunity to voice that support in rather unexpected places. In August 1973, for example, he was invited to speak before the National Medical Association, an organization of black doctors formed in the days when the American Medical Association did not admit black doctors to membership. The assembled doctors expected the congressman to talk about health care for the poor, which he did, but he saw no reason why doctors should be uninvolved in voter registration. Outlining the provisions of the bill, he suggested that if it were passed, doctors could keep a supply of postcards in their waiting rooms. In that way, every doctor's waiting room would also become a voter registration station. He supported many other "pro-people" measures. Some people felt at first that he was being pro-black, but during that first congressional session they began to realize that he was not so easily categorized.

In October 1973 Vice-President Spiro T. Agnew resigned, after pleading *nolo contendere* (no contest) to charges of federal income tax evasion. It was merely the latest in a growing list of blots on the record of the Nixon Administration. Back during the 1972 presidential campaign, five men had been caught breaking into the Democratic headquarters in Washington's Watergate Hotel. Although no one had yet been able to connect Richard Nixon and his advisers directly with the burglars, there was much suspicion, and by the time Agnew resigned so had several of the President's top aides. Many people in Congress felt that the President himself might eventually be forced to resign and that whoever succeeded Spiro T. Agnew as Vice-President might well end up being President.

The President appointed Gerald R. Ford, a Republican senator from Michigan, as his new Vice-President. It was then up to Congress to confirm the appointment. Ford was subjected to some tough questioning by the members of Congress, among them black members who were concerned about Ford's poor voting record on civil rights measures. Andrew Young was well aware of Ford's poor civil rights record, but he believed there were other factors to consider. As he explained, "Gerald Ford had voted against everything I had been for, yet I found being around him a good experience. I decided that here was a guy I wanted to give a chance. He was certainly better than Reagan or any of the other alternatives at the time. [If Nixon were to resign, it was expected that California Governor Ronald Reagan would run for President in 1976.] Besides, Atlanta was going to need to work very closely with the next administration." Not only was Andrew Young the only member of the Congressional Black Caucus who voted to confirm Ford's appointment, he actually made a speech in the House supporting Ford's nomination as Vice-President.

The House Judiciary Committee began hearings on the impeachment, or removal from office, of President Nixon in November 1973, and on July 27, 1974, the committee voted that there were grounds for impeachment. On the evening of August 8, 1974, President Nixon resigned and Gerald R. Ford became President. Among Ford's first acts was to grant a "full, free and absolute" pardon to Richard Nixon, an act that infuriated many people, including every black legislator save one. That one was Andrew Young. It seemed to him that there was no point in further prosecution of Richard Nixon. He had not liked the man, but he was not the vengeful sort. Andrew Young never allowed himself to feel bitterness; when an unpleasant situation was over, he put it out of his mind. To him, Ford's pardon of Nixon was in keeping with biblical teaching to forgive. "It's the preacher in me coming out," Andrew explained with a chuckle.

Also in keeping with biblical teaching was the granting of amnesty to the young men who had left the country in order to avoid being drafted to fight in Vietnam. Many young men had done so in the late 1960s and early 1970s. They had gone to Canada or to the Scandinavian countries, leaving their family and friends behind. By 1974, U.S. troops had been pulled out of Vietnam and no one was being drafted, and many of the young men in exile outside the country longed to return. They dared not return, however, because they faced criminal charges in the United States—prison sentences in some cases, or periods of work to make up for the service they had not performed in the military. In August 1974, not long after he had pardoned former President Nixon, President Ford announced that he would grant amnesty, or pardon, to all the young draft evaders who wished to return to the country. In this decision, he was supported by all in the Congressional Black Caucus, although some members were rather grudging in their support. Ford's action justified Andrew Young's support of him. Andrew Young had been able to see past Ford's political philosophy, which differed radically from his, and to see Ford as a basically good and generous man.

During 1974, Young voted with the majority of other Democrats in the House for the first bill to impose federal environmental controls on the strip mining of coal, and against amendments proposed by Republicans that would weaken the bill. In the midst of the fuel crisis in early 1974, when gas and oil prices rose drastically and drivers had to wait in long lines to get gasoline at service stations, he joined with two other representatives and three senators to urge the Federal Trade Commission to investigate the advertising practices of the major oil companies. The companies, Young and the others charged, were running advertisements aimed at turning aside public discontent with high prices and shortages, claiming that they were doing all they could to improve conditions. They wanted the FTC to require the companies to supply proof of the claims they made in their ads.

A number of groups make a point of keeping track of individual congresspersons' voting records on various issues and reporting their findings to the public. Some of them are: Americans for Democratic Action (ADA), the Committee on Political Education (COPE), the League of Conservation Voters (LCV), the National Association of Businessmen (NAB), the American Security Council (ASC), and the Americans for Constitutional Action (ACA). Andrew Young got consistently high ratings from the liberal organizations like the ADA and the conservation organizations like the LCV (he was one of only eight Democrats to receive a perfect rating from the LCV in 1973). He got consistently low ratings from the conservative organizations like the NAB and the ACA (he got a zero rating from the ACA in 1974 and a 4 in 1973). There is no rating for respect, regardless of philosophy, but if there had been, Andrew Young would probably have rated high on nearly every list.

By the time he had to run for re-election, Young had established a reputation in Congress as a conscientious representative of his constituency, a man of character and intelligence and genuine concern for the problems of people, no matter what their race. He had approached politics as he had approached his work in the civil rights struggle, based on the Gandhian philosophy. As he explains, "It says we all inherit a point of view, a set of obligations. When they come into conflict, it's not that one is right and the other wrong. There's a new situation, and you sit down together and work out a solution to it."

During that first term in office, he had been approached by a group of black leaders seeking additional federal funding for the black land-grant colleges. Young could have made a public appeal to Congress for help, but he knew he would risk inviting the resistance of a lot of conservative congressmen, whose constituencies would expect them to be against the additional funding. So Young went to the chairman of the Agricultural Appropriations Subcommittee. Although the man was known as a die-hard segregationist, Young was able to persuade him to include money for the colleges in a bill that was then going through Congress. The bill passed, and the colleges got additional funds without the matter's becoming a big issue.

His fellow congressmen had responded well to Young's methods. They knew he kept his promises, was open to other ideas, acted out of a strong sense of morality. He and Barbara Jordan, both freshmen and the only southern black representatives, were among the few members of Congress who got the respect of silence on the House floor when they rose to speak.

Said Charles Wilson, Democratic representative from Texas, "He's the best bridge between the various factions. If it has anything to do with black-white relations, if you need balance on a study group or a committee or the like, you almost always go to Andy Young, often first. He's a man of sweet reason."

Andrew Young had also earned the respect of many of the whites in Atlanta who had been suspicious of him at the beginning of his term. They might not agree with the way he voted at times (the white businessmen were well aware of his rating of 17 for 1974 by the National Association of Businessmen), but they were convinced that he voted out of reason rather than political or racial prejudice. And they were also aware that he was a great booster of Atlanta. Back in April, he had told a New York *Times* reporter that Atlanta was the best city in the United States for black professionals, and he had voiced similar sentiments to reporters from other influential publications. In the opinion of Atlanta's businessmen, every time a black, former civil rights leader said something good about Atlanta it boosted the city's reputation immeasurably.

Andrew Young was unopposed in the 1974 Democratic primary and won the general election easily, polling 69,221 votes to his Republican opponent's 27,397. By that time, blacks constituted 44 percent of the voters in the district and no one was equating the election of a black to the fall of Western civilization. In fact, Young had never known he had so many friends. "Alabama's white politicians were frank," he was fond of telling audiences. "They called us niggers. A year or two later, when blacks in a community got 30 percent of the vote, we became nigras. Later on still, at about 40 percent, we were either Nee-grows or colored people, and by the time we had gotten a clear majority of the vote, the pols [politicians] had adopted us as their black brothers." He would chuckle as he said it, and audiences black and white would laugh with him, because even the whites understood that the statement was made entirely without rancor. He was simply stating a political truth.

In January 1975 Young returned to Congress with relish.

No longer a freshman congressman, he exercised his new power by getting himself appointed to the powerful House Rules Committee, a committee on which very few representatives managed to get a seat after only two years. Not only that, but Andrew Young happened to be the first black ever to serve on that committee.

He also added a new activity to his already busy schedule. He decided to help the new freshman Democratic representatives. He remembered how hard it had been for him to learn the facts of legislative life, and he was willing to share his experiences. With seven other incumbent representatives, he held a series of meetings with 30 of the 75 newly elected Democrats in the House. Such meetings were not new, but Young and the others established a precedent; for the first time, the sessions were open to the press. Those freshman congressmen were lucky to have someone like Andrew Young to share his experiences with them. After two years in the House, he had known all the frustrations of a freshman representative, and he was still optimistic—not falsely optimistic because now he had a "position" to preserve, but genuinely optimistic that as a congressman he could really help people.

"He enjoyed the *process* of getting something to happen and working very closely with people who had differing political views," says Jean Young. "He liked being able to work with people and getting something to happen because of it. Sometimes the length of time it would take would bother him. And he was bothered by the fact that even though the issues seemed so clear sometimes they could become so very muddled. And sometimes he was frustrated at how difficult it was to make *big* things happen. But he really could see some progress in the little things that would happen."

During that second term in Congress, Young supported bills increasing the minimum wage and extending coverage to domestic workers, broadening the food stamp program and establishing a federal day care program. He introduced a bill outlining a comprehensive national health care program and one that would make the banks of the polluted Chattahoochee River into Georgia's first national park. He had consistently voted against military aid to the South Vietnamese regime, but after the fall of that government in April 1975 he voted for emergency humanitarian and evacuation aid.

In February 1975 he and Massachusetts Representative Michael Harrington joined to urge the Senate Foreign Relations Committee to reject the nomination of Nathaniel Davis for Assistant State Secretary for African Affairs. Both Young and Harrington agreed with other critics of Davis that the man had been linked with CIA operations against the government of the late President of Chile, Salvador Allende. In 1973, Allende's government had been overthrown by the military of that country. Many people suspected that the U.S. Central Intelligence Agency had been involved in the overthrow, although the CIA denied any complicity. Andrew Young, among others, felt the CIA had no business interfering in the affairs of another country and he did not want anyone suspected of having been part of that kind of interference to hold such a key position in U.S. relations with Africa.

Young kept in close touch with the African embassies in the United States and, as a congressman, made several trips to Africa, either to attend meetings or on good-will missions. In November 1975 he and Martin Luther King's widow, Coretta Scott King, traveled together on such a good-will mission to Lagos, Nigeria. He made his first visit to South Africa, on an unofficial basis, in 1974.

South Africa's population was overwhelmingly black, but its government and its economic structure were overwhelmingly white. The minority white population controlled all government, business, and commerce as well as the rigid system of racial segregation called apartheid. Under apartheid, black

South Africans had to live in designated areas, could not travel without passes, and had even fewer rights than southern black Americans in the most segregated areas before the civil rights movement. Andrew Young had read a lot about South Africa and had considered the idea that a civil rights movement such as had improved conditions for blacks in the United States might work there. But he had never visited the country. Then, in 1974, black tennis star Arthur Ashe suggested that Young accompany him there.

Andrew Young and Arthur Ashe were good friends. They played tennis together and shared many other interests. When Ashe married, he would ask Young to perform the ceremony. When Ashe won the Wimbledon Tennis Tournament, Young gave a reception for him at the Rayburn Office Building in Washington.

"Arthur was very intrigued by South African politics and he and Andrew had had long conversations on the subject," Jean Young recalls. "So when Arthur decided to go over there and play in a tournament he said to Andrew, 'Why don't you come with me so you can really talk with the people, get a feel for what is going on there and give them a feel for what is going on in the United States?' So Andrew went.

"Over there, Andrew said the one thing he'd really like to do is meet Robert Sobukwe, because he was sort of the Martin Luther King of South Africa. Sobukwe had spent about eight or nine years in solitary confinement somewhere and was still under confinement and enjoyed only limited movement."

Andrew Young would reminisce about that meeting with Robert Sobukwe when he visited South Africa as U.S. Ambassador to the United Nations three years later: "I went down to Kimberly to visit Robert Sobukwe, and he was not long out of your prisons, and the thing that amazed me was that there wasn't a trace of bitterness in this man. And after about an hour's conversation I said, 'Look, how can you live through what you've been through and still give a sensitive analysis of the people who put you through it?' and he said, 'Well, it's because I know that we will prevail.' He said, 'I was reading about your country and I read *Uncle Tom's Cabin*, and I decided that if you chaps could live through that and come to where you have now come, there's no question that we will be able to overcome in South Africa as well."

Young was very impressed with Sobukwe. "So," says Jean Young, "Andrew said in his way, 'If there's anything I can do for you in the United States, I wish you'd let me know.' He was completely sincere, and so Sobukwe responded that what concerned him most at that time was that his children have an opportunity to get a decent education. And so two months later we had them in the United States with us."

Andrew Young does not offer help when he does not mean it. He wanted to help Robert Sobukwe and Sobukwe, trusting Young's word, accepted the offer. Dinilesizwe Sobukwe, seventeen, and his sister, Miliswa Sobukwe, eighteen, were welcomed into the Young family.

"They're marvelous kids," says Jean Young. "I think it was something of a culture shock for them to come to the United States after having lived so long under the rigidity of the South African regime, but they're doing well."

Back in the United States and in Congress, Andrew Young continued to represent the people of Atlanta as he had promised and as he thought best. By that time, he and Jean had bought a house in Washington, because they felt it was time to have a real home base there. Young was overwhelmingly returned to Congress in the November 1976 election, so it looked as if he would be there for a while. Then, too, he had children whom he wanted to be close to.

Speaking of those years when Andrew was in Congress, Jean Young says, "I liked it. It was a comfortable life. He was probably *with* the kids more during that period than during the civil rights struggle when everything was somewhat chaotic. And he was happy, enjoying the opportunity to let the country know what the average person felt strongly about. He had a health bill, an environmental bill, and other kinds of bills that responded specifically to the needs of people."

Shortly, however, Congressman Andrew Young would leave that comfortable life for yet a new challenge.

9 / A "New South" Alliance

"I remember flying in a helicopter down Georgia's Chatta-hoochee River with Jimmy Carter and Scoop Jackson [Henry Jackson, Democratic senator from Washington State, who was thinking of running for President in 1976] and listening to Jimmy, who was Governor then, discuss environmental issues with Scoop," wrote Andrew Young early in 1976. "He not only held his own but took Scoop on in energy questions as well. Jimmy is like that. He sized up all the presidential prospects who came through Georgia while he was governor, and de-cided they didn't know any more than he did and that he could outwork any of them, so why not run for President?"

On the face of it, that idea seemed as farfetched as Andrew Young's idea, back in 1970, that he could be elected to Con-gress. A candidate from the Deep South had never been elected President. The most southerly state from which a President had come was South Carolina, the birthplace of Andrew Jackson (Andrew Young's namesake, coincidentally), who had served from 1829 to 1837. As if that were not enough against him, Jimmy Carter was an unknown. He had never served in Congress. His only political credentials were as governor of Georgia. But Jimmy Carter was also an optimistic man, and believed that if he worked hard enough he could achieve his goal, to be elected President of the United States in 1976.

Young was invited to a Carter strategy session as early as 1974, well before Carter announced that he was running. One of the purposes of the session was to identify issues, and Young agreed to attend the meeting on that basis. He was not at all sure that Carter would make a good President, but he realized he should not miss the chance to establish the importance of certain issues in which he was interested, for what better forum could there be for such issues than a presidential candidate's platform?

Some of Carter's aides expected Andrew to push for black issues, which they did not feel Carter needed. They were pleasantly surprised when the congressman emphasized his concern for the world economic crisis. He mentioned that a healthy economy would be good for black people, but his emphasis was on what would be good for Americans in general. By putting his emphasis on the larger picture, Young was not trying to be a wolf in sheep's clothing. As his record in Congress had already shown, he did not confine himself merely to black issues but addressed issues concerning all the American people that would also benefit blacks in the long run. Having made his feelings known to Carter and his aides, he left the meeting without committing himself to being a part of the campaign Carter was planning.

Over the next year or so, Carter continued to solicit advice from Young. In the area of foreign relations, for example, it was Young who suggested a change in U.S. relations with the Third World, a designation given to those developing and usually needy nations that are not aligned with either the communist or the capitalist countries. In the past, the United States had been cool to those countries. In addition to his genuine concern for their people, Young believed that the Third World, with its oil and other rich natural resources, would assume ever greater importance in the world community and that the United States would do well to develop friendships there. He also felt that Carter should take a firm stand against apartheid in South Africa. Eventually, Carter would incorporate Young's views in his platform.

Carter announced his candidacy for President in December 1974, the second man to announce (liberal Democrat Morris K. Udall of Arizona had announced earlier). Although Young continued to watch Carter closely, he was hoping that Massachusetts senator Edward Kennedy, the last surviving Kennedy brother, would elect to run. Barring a Kennedy candidacy, he intended to support a proven liberal Democrat such as Udall or Walter Mondale of Minnesota.

"The most formal dinner we ever had in Atlanta was for Walter Mondale, before he became Vice-President," says Jean Young. Andrew had invited him down to speak at a campaign breakfast given by local businessmen, and Jimmy Carter gave the introduction for Mondale. They had never met before, but Young knew them both and had great respect for them. "I was impressed with Mondale and excited about his candidacy for President. . . . That evening we had a roast-beef buffet dinner for Mondale and invited about forty people from the community, along with our friends. We set up tables in the basement of our home, and everyone served himself."

Actually, Andrew Young and Jimmy Carter had a number of things in common, and Young had considered them. First and foremost, both were southerners, and that was a bond that was far more important than people in other parts of the country could understand. Both had grown up primarily with children of the other race, Andrew Young in the Cleveland Street neighborhood in New Orleans and Jimmy Carter in Plains, Georgia, which had more black people than white. Both were religious men, Young a minister and Carter a self-acknowledged "born-again Christian." And both, interestingly enough, had similar families. Jimmy and Rosalynn Carter had had three sons and, after a long time, a daughter. Andrew and Jean Young had had three daughters, and, after a long time, a son. These similarities were not enough to cause Young to support the Carter candidacy, but they reinforced his interest and he followed that candidacy closely. In those early days, he concentrated on his work in Congress and left the presidential campaign to the candidates.

What prompted Young to get involved in that campaign was the candidacy of former Alabama governor George Wallace. Wallace, who had run strongly in the South in the 1972 presidential campaign, had changed his tune since he had reluctantly agreed to see the delegation from the Selma to Montgomery march back in 1965. Bowing to the pressure of political reality, he no longer spoke of segregating "niggers" and was working hard to curry the favor of black voters. Young was willing to accept the new Wallace up to a point, but he did not want Wallace to be accepted as the voice of the New South. A more progressive southern candidate should be that spokesman, and the logical one was Jimmy Carter.

The real test would come in March 1976 in the Florida Democratic primary. In Young's opinion, the Florida primary had been a "burying ground" for progressive candidates back in 1972, for George Wallace had won decisively there that year and Republican incumbent Richard Nixon had, Andrew Young believed, viewed the Wallace win as a mandate to pursue ever more conservative policies after he was re-elected that

November. So, months before the Florida primary, Young began publicly supporting Carter. He praised Carter and recommended that other Democratic candidates stay out of the Florida primary so as not to split the moderate and liberal votes. He was not committed to Carter as a presidential candidate so much as he was committed to beating George Wallace in the most important southern primary. He informed Carter that his support could be counted on only through the Florida election.

Having committed himself to Carter in the Florida primary, Young made good on his promise by speaking on the candidate's behalf before black audiences and white liberal audiences. His message was simple: that Carter was a good man, that his record on civil rights might not be a glowing one, but that it was certainly better than Wallace's, that if a New South was really emerging, its people would have to cast aside the symbols of the Old South, like George Wallace. In the meantime Carter and his aides worked hard in Florida, taking a center or moderate position on issues and building a strong organization in the state. All that work paid off on primary day. Carter won 34 percent of the vote to Wallace's 31 percent. Carter received nearly three quarters of all the votes cast by blacks; without that 75,000 votes or so, he would have come in second or third. He also received majorities of the votes cast by people under 25, blue-collar workers, and liberals.

Carter's victory over Wallace had not been a stunning one, but it had been a victory, and as far as Andrew Young was concerned that was enough. What he had to do now was to decide whether or not to continue supporting Carter. Udall, whom he had favored earlier, had not fared particularly well, had not even been among the top three vote-getters. Walter Mondale had dropped out of the race.

The outcome of the Massachusetts primary, which Jimmy Carter did not enter, helped Young make his decision. Henry

"Scoop" Jackson had won it, and his victory had surprised many people who had thought that liberal Indiana Senator Birch Bayh would be the victor. Not only was Young surprised, he was also concerned. Jackson was against busing. He supported the policies of U.N. Ambassador Daniel Patrick Moynihan, who had called the U.N. a "theater of the absurd" and who favored a "get tough" method of dealing with Third World nations. He was much too conservative for Young's tastes, and Young feared his victory signaled trends and possibilities he did not like. As he wrote in April 1976, "The result [of the Jackson victory] was: 1) the demise of Birch Bayh, the liberal who had the best chance of beating Jackson in New York; 2) the resurgence of cold-war foreign policy and a dangerous swing to the right internationally; 3) the potential of a Jackson boom sweeping the big industrial states and creating a very negative national mood in both domestic and foreign policy; and 4) the possibility of a private deal with Wallace that would give Jackson the nomination and Wallace the influence behind the scenes, though not a place on the ticket." It seemed to Young that the only Democratic candidate who could minimize Jackson's support in the upcoming New York primary was Jimmy Carter.

Young thought long and hard about Jimmy Carter. The candidate had grown up with black people and seemed to get along well with them. He had quite a few black people on his staff, probably more than all the other candidates put together. Before he had ever gotten into politics he had refused membership in the White Citizens Council. In his first elective office he had blocked the transfer of public school funds to segregated academies in Sumter County, Georgia. As Governor of Georgia he had reformed the state's terrible prison system, deputized every high school principal in the state as a voting registrar, and appointed more blacks to positions on various state commissions and agencies than had ever been on them before. He had fought for environmental issues and worked to end the "waiting week" which was required before workers could receive unemployment compensation. He was able to organize efficiently and he enjoyed solving problems. His appeal was personal rather than ideological. He enjoyed discovering effective solutions to "people" problems.

"I'm a romantic and an idealist, so it was very difficult for me to ignore such a moral and political success story," Young wrote that April. "Admittedly, these alone do not qualify a man to be President of the United States. They do qualify him as a representative of the New South and a voice capable of ending the Wallace myth, which led politicians of both parties to turn to the right. The principles of tolerance and fairness led me into a relationship with Jimmy Carter, but it is hard political reality that keeps me there."

Young became the first nationally known elected official, black or white, and the first important Georgia politician to support Jimmy Carter's candidacy. He was taking a gamble. Carter was still an unknown nationally. His opponents, Democrats and Republicans alike, were fond of asking, "Jimmy Who?" Second, and more important, Andrew Young did not know Jimmy Carter all that well. He seemed a good, trustworthy man, but Young could not be sure he would not change his position on the issues and adopt positions Young could not support. Young made his commitment more out of faith than anything else.

Young became part of Carter's "inner circle." He was asked to visit Plains frequently. He was also given drafts of some of Carter's speeches and asked to comment on them. His advice was solicited primarily on issues affecting black people, and because of his long-standing interest in Africa he also had considerable input into the parts of the Carter platform that had to do with U.S. relations with the Third World. Perhaps

Ambassador Young meets with President Carter and Secretary of State Cyrus Vance at the White House. Because he had brought in the black vote, Young was called the individual most responsible for the success of Carter's presidential campaign.

he was of greatest help in the area of day-to-day campaigning. There were many other states where important primaries were to be held, and in order for a candidate to be a serious contender he had to make a good showing in a majority of them. To make that good showing, he had to spark the interest and win the confidence of many Democratic voters. The northern primaries would be particularly important. Voters in those states would be suspicious of Carter merely because he was a southerner. Blacks and white liberals would be suspicious of him because he was a white southerner. Few others could allay the suspicions of these groups as well as a black, southern veteran of the civil rights movement named Andrew Young.

Even Andrew Young had to work hard to undo the potentially damaging effects of a statement Carter made in April. Speaking before a predominantly white, working-class audience, Carter made an off-the-cuff remark about the right of individuals to resist "black intrusion" and "alien groups" and to preserve the "ethnic purity of neighborhoods." The remark was widely reported and it angered many blacks and particularly white liberals, just the groups on whom Young was concentrating. In his opinion, Carter's remark could not have been more ill-advised, even though he suspected it was Carter's way of reassuring working-class whites that they need not fear him as too liberal a candidate. Publicly, Young denounced the remark, calling Carter's choice of words "awful" and "loaded with Hitlerian connotations." He had to make such a denunciation to maintain his own credibility with the groups who had criticized the remark. Privately, he recommended that Carter make a public apology for the statement and that he further remedy the situation by making more statements on urban policy and unemployment. Carter followed Young's recommendations and the furor over the "ethnic purity" remark died down.

In primary states across the country, Young traveled to speak on Carter's behalf. He spoke at churches to audiences of middle-income blacks. He spoke at fund-raisers to white northern liberals in cities like New York. He spoke before labor groups, both black and white. Back during the days when he had set up training programs for future black officeholders, he had kept a file with the names and addresses of the people who had passed through those programs. He also had lists of all the black clergymen in the major southern cities, from his days wth SCLC. He used these lists to reach a wide number of people both to assure Carter a hearing and to launch voter registration drives. He was, in his view, merely "opening the doors" to these constituencies for Carter. In the view of most observers, however, he also "qualified" them for Carter. He allayed their suspicions of the candidate from Georgia. After all, the man could hardly be a racist and have such strong support from Andrew Young. If Andrew Young said he was good, then he must be good.

Young was not the only important black to support Carter. Ben Brown, a Georgia assemblyman with wide contacts, was another. So was Martin Luther King, Sr., the father of the slain civil rights leader. But most black leaders had a "wait and see" attitude about Carter. They could not quite trust the white Georgian. Julian Bond was one, but there were many more. As Bond explained, "Andy and people like him seem to have left their bitterness behind them. I like to keep my bitterness out front, because it keeps the issues in focus."

What bothered a lot of other black politicians was that Young was helping Carter for almost purely altruistic reasons. He wanted a Democratic President who would be committed to improving the lives of Americans, whether through jobs or environmental controls or a system of national health care, or becoming more friendly with Third World nations that controlled important world resources. He had never asked, "What's in it for me?" or even, "What's in it for black people?" The others thought he should at least secure some assurance from Carter that he would appoint a black to his Cabinet if he were elected President. But Andrew Young was helping because he wanted to, not because he wanted something in return. He did not want a Cabinet appointment or a White House staff job for himself, and he did not feel he had to secure guarantees from Carter that blacks would be represented in his administration. "It won't be a *cause*," he explained. "There won't be special committees and special commissions to find and appoint blacks. It will be natural. There'll just be a lot of black folks where they've never been before, on regulatory commissions and such. His first appointments to commissions will often be black, but without a lot of fanfare. That's the way he did it in Georgia."

Largely because of the help of Andrew Young, Carter's primary victories began to pile up. Heavy support from black voters proved decisive in key primaries. In Michigan, for example, it was the black vote that helped him beat Morris Udall. No longer was anyone saying, "Jimmy Who?" By late spring, George Wallace had realized he had no chance at all at the Democratic presidential nomination and, like a growing number of southern Democrats, he had joined the Carter coalition. Being in the same camp with George Wallace was a little hard for Young to take, but he was able to put aside his memories of George Wallace the rabid segregationist and view the man as one who had bowed to political and social reality.

Speaking as a southern black, he explained, "We've had a lot of experience with converted bigots and we know we can trust them. It's not just an intellectual commitment with them. They proved themselves in a personal struggle, often against family and tradition. . . . They don't chicken out—and some people do, when it comes to housing in New York and busing in Boston." The difference between white southern former segregationists and northern white liberals, Young has often said, is that the southern whites want to solve problems *with* blacks while the northern whites want to solve problems *for* them.

Over the months of campaigning, Young got to know Jimmy Carter quite well. They conferred almost daily by telephone, not just about racial issues but about many others. They traveled together on campaign tours. They did not become "runnin' buddies," as Young puts it, but they developed a deep respect for each other. Carter even consulted Young on possible vice-presidential running mates.

Young suggested several names. One was Walter Mondale, the senator from Minnesota who had been a candidate for President for a brief time. Another was Peter Rodino, a congressman from New Jersey and the chairman of the House Judiciary Committee. Young suggested Rodino because he felt that Carter did not have enough support in the Italian-American communities. Rodino graciously declined the offer to be considered, but he did ask Carter if he could make the speech nominating him for President at the Democratic Nominating Convention in June. It was an honor Andrew Young was supposed to have had, but Young did not insist on it. He told Carter to let Rodino give the speech, for it might still help attract support from Italian-Americans.

At the convention in June, Young made one of the speeches seconding Carter's nomination. "I'm ready to lay down the burden of race," he told the delegates, "and Jimmy Carter comes from a part of the country which, whether you know it or not, has done just that." Martin Luther King, Sr., also made a seconding speech, and after all the many speeches the actual balloting did not take long. Many times there are two popular candidates and several ballots are necessary to decide the party's nominee. Not so in 1976. Jimmy Carter won the nomination on the first ballot. A year earlier hardly anyone outside Georgia even knew him, and he openly expressed his debt to Andrew Young for his almost meteoric rise, saying Young was the individual to whom he was most indebted for his political support. If Carter won the presidential election in November, Andrew Jackson Young, Jr., would probably have more direct influence on government than any black in American history. And he would have achieved that position of power and influence without having made any important enemies along the way.

"A campaign grows so big, it grows so fast," Young said

shortly after the Democratic convention. "The small group of us that started out two years ago now has expanded, and I don't know who they are. There are all kinds of people coming in, and at this point you get a little nervous about who is going to have what influence." One of the people who made Andrew nervous was Charles Kirbo, a Georgian who had become one of Carter's closest advisers. In an interview with the Los Angeles *Times* Washington Bureau staff not long after the convention, he described Kirbo as an "old-fashioned Georgia cracker." Asked about that characterization later, he pleaded that the occasion had been an "early morning breakfast" and qualified his statement, saying he did not know Kirbo very well and that the few experiences he'd had with Kirbo had been good, but that he was concerned about the man's conservative background.

Another man who made him nervous was Zbigncw Brzezinski, whom Carter had taken on as a foreign policy adviser. Young did not know Brzezinski and did not know what his foreign policy priorities were. Young wondered what kind of input he himself would have now. He made no bones about his feeling that the United States should press for racial equality in South Africa "very far, very fast." He did not know how Brzezinski felt about U.S. policy in Africa.

But though he was nervous, he did not lose his commitment to Carter and his campaign. There was much hard work to be done to win the presidency from the incumbent, Republican Gerald Ford, and everyone on the Carter team worked very hard. Andrew Young mobilized a massive door-to-door registration drive in the inner cities and managed to get some three million new voters, predominantly Democrats. In November, the years of hard work paid off. James Earl Carter defeated Gerald Ford by slightly more than 1,700,000 votes and became the first President ever to be elected from the Deep South.

All the while Andrew Young had been campaigning for

Jimmy Carter he had not neglected his other duties. He spent as much time as he could with his family and made a point of giving Bo the attention the little boy needed. He visited the children of Martin Luther King, Jr., something he had done regularly since his friend's death. He even preached an occasional sermon at an Atlanta church. He wanted to keep his hand in and was proud of the fact that students of the art of preaching rated him high in ability to move a congregation.

He was still a congressman, and he had not allowed the Carter campaign to cause him to neglect his responsibilities on Capitol Hill. His style changed not at all during that time. He continued to prefer quiet negotiation and to be sensitive to the feelings of the other side. In early August 1976, the House Rules Committee met to consider a bill to place North Carolina's New River under the protection of the Wild and Scenic Rivers system. The bill was a controversial one, and there had been much lobbying on behalf of both sides. The tense atmosphere had not been helped by the behavior of Stephen Neal, a freshman congressman from North Carolina and one of the principal sponsors of the bill. He had publicly criticized the members of the Rules Committee who were opposed to the bill, which was not very smart considering that those same members would now vote on it. When Neal appeared as a witness before the committee, he was asked to retract his statements. He refused, saying, "I did not mean to impugn the motives of all members of this committee."

Hearing this statement, Young, who supported the bill, groaned to himself. If Neal wasn't careful, he would kill the bill's chances for sure. "*Any* members, *any* . . ." he whispered loudly to the freshman congressman. When the hearing recessed, Young and a few others took Neal aside and gave him a brief course in congressional decorum. When the hearing resumed, Neal apologized for his remarks. The committee voted the bill out to the House floor.

To Andrew Young, that small victory was important, just as were the other small victories and the few larger ones he had been able to accomplish as a congressman. His constituents seemed satisfied, too, and on the same day that Jimmy Carter had been elected President, Andrew had been overwhelmingly re-elected to his third term in Congress. There were many who predicted that if he were patient enough he might eventually become the first Speaker of the House or even the first black Senator from Georgia.

In the middle of November, President-elect Carter chose Andrew Young to represent the new administration at a meeting of American and African leaders in Lesotho, South Africa. The trip only served to bolster Young's feeling that a strong U.S. policy in support of majority rule in South Africa was absolutely necessary, that if it could be achieved nonviolently the United States, for trying, would earn an excellent reputation in the rest of the Third World and in return would get support from those countries on energy issues and the Middle East. Returning to the United States, Young reported on the meeting to Carter, who was impressed by his grasp of the African situation. Shortly thereafter, Carter offered Young the post of United States Ambassador to the United Nations, which he had decided to make a Cabinet-level post. The appointment of the first black person in history to an American President's Cabinet was announced publicly on December 16.

Most black politicians and most of Young's close friends were against his accepting the appointment. John Lewis, former executive director of SNCC, told him he would be able to help black people more by staying in Congress and taking advantage of his closeness to the President to push for domestic legislation. Julian Bond, alluding to the fact that black people tend to consider the U.N. as not very powerful or important, quipped, "I can't imagine Andy going to the U.N. to succeed

Andrew Young knew he was taking a risk when he accepted the post as U.S. Ambassador to the U.N. Not a single friend or adviser thought he should leave Congress.

Pearl Bailey." Hosea Williams, one of the SCLC leaders who had been through the civil rights struggle with Young, could find no humor in the situation at all. He saw the appointment as positively subversive, a "political kidnapping" engineered "by Atlanta's white power structure to retake political control of Atlanta." Although most would not use quite the same language, there were other black Georgians who feared it would be difficult to get another black elected from the 56 percent white Fifth Congressional District and that Andrew's giving up the seat would be tantamount to giving it back to white politicians.

Then there was the matter of the position itself. Black people were not the only Americans who did not think the U.N. or its ambassadors had much influence in the world. Neither it nor they carried much weight in policy matters. Many former U.S. Ambassadors to the U.N. had been terribly frustrated in the job, feeling they were unable to act independently of the U.S. State Department and that they had no real say in U.S. foreign policy.

Andrew Young had considered all these points, as well as many others. He never took a major step without carefully considering it. While Carter kept urging him to accept the appointment, calling him several times on the telephone, inviting him to Plains to discuss it, even calling Jean Young, Andrew refused to make a hasty decision.

"You know," says Jean Young, "every time Andrew has made a decision it hasn't been made lightly. It has been made with a great deal of thought and contemplation and soul-searching. I knew he did not want to leave Congress. But the more he thought about it, the more he realized that this was perhaps an opportunity to have a voice on the world scene that might not occur again in the near future.

"He'd always been interested in the U.N., and since childhood he'd had a tremendous admiration for Ralph Bunche.

He'd thought of maybe sometime, 'way in the future, relating to the U.N. as an elder statesman—he had that kind of image of himself somewhere in the back of his mind, and he'd expressed it to me on occasion. But he'd never spoken in terms of being an ambassador or any very active role. Just sort of hidden somewhere was the idea that when he was in his seventies he might serve in some kind of advisory capacity.

"So he was very reluctant to think of himself in those terms *now*. He felt ill-prepared for it in some respects, felt perhaps he wasn't really ready for it. But the more he thought about it the more he realized that there are moments in history when you have to take advantage of whatever you're confronted with and go into it and do what you're called on to do. And it was out of that context that he responded and said, 'Well, maybe this is what I do need to be doing at this moment, because the opportunity may never come again.'

"It was the right decision, but it was a difficult one for him. There were thousands of telephone calls, but there was not one person who said, 'This is what you should be doing.' "

Major presidential appointments must be confirmed by Congress, and on January 25, 1977, Andrew Young appeared at a confirmation hearing before the Senate Foreign Relations Committee. In reply to their probing questions, he spoke as he truly felt. He recommended that the United States establish normal diplomatic relations with the Socialist Republic of Vietnam. He also reiterated his statements about the advisability of the U.S. moving forcefully for an end to apartheid in South Africa and Rhodesia. In that light, he said, he felt the United States should stop importing chrome from the two African countries, for not only did trading with them indicate a tacit acceptance of apartheid by the United States but also it went against United Nations sanctions. His appointment was unanimously endorsed by the committee, and approved by the full Senate shortly thereafter.

Thus, the forty-four-year-old first black United States Ambassador to the United Nations awaited only the formal presentation of his credentials to the Secretary-General. He was aware that he was a "first,'" but he had either been or been involved in other "firsts." Although there were ways in which he believed himself to be unprepared for his new job, there were also ways in which he believed he was uniquely prepared.

Once, speaking of his experience in world affairs, he said, "I guess I began to see that in the world white people are afraid of black people, and black people—maybe for good reasons—don't trust white people and, more important, don't understand them. Maybe the single most important dynamic in today's foreign relations is racism." Andrew Young had a lot of experience with racism, with fearful whites and distrustful blacks. He had been able to be a "reconciler of men," as he liked to describe himself, during the civil rights struggle and to a certain extent even in Congress. He hoped he would be able to play the same role in the world arena.

But given the American attitude toward the United Nations, given the traditional barriers to power and influence that U.S. Ambassadors to the U.N. had found blocking their way to real effectiveness, would he be able to play that role? He had accepted the appointment only after being assured by Carter that he would have an input in foreign policy. But his friends still wondered whether he had done the right thing. Said one, "I think the most frustrating thing in the world would be to see this great and good man walking through the corridors of the U.N., hailed by everybody, beloved by everybody, but having absolutely no impact at all."

10 / Man with a Mission

Andrew Young formally presented his credentials to the Secretary-General of the United Nations, Kurt Waldheim, on January 31, 1977. Then he paused to look around him at the great edifice that had been erected with so much hope a quarter-century before. Every nation in the world was represented here, from the largest and richest to the smallest and poorest. It was a forum like none that had ever existed in history before, and yet it had come to be regarded as a joke by most Americans. One reason was that the United States no longer enjoyed the influence it had once wielded there. When the U.N. was chartered in 1945, there were 51 member nations; by 1977 there were 147. The majority of nations that had joined since 1945 were small, underdeveloped, and non-white, but in most sections of the organization their votes were

In the fall of 1977, Andrew Young, shown here with his parents, returned to Dillard University in New Orleans to accept an honorary degree. He had spent his freshman year of college at Dillard.

given equal weight with that of the United States, and with increasing frequency they had not voted the same way the United States had. About twenty could be considered part of the Western bloc; about twenty others could be counted on to vote with the Soviet Union, and the rest voted quite independently.

Another reason was that the U.N. was considered unsuccessful in seriously addressing world problems. Too often, the communist countries had used it not as a place for finding common ground with other nations but as a propaganda platform for speeches to be reported at home. The organization had never been intended to replace individual countries' Departments of State or Ministries of Foreign Affairs, but over the preceding decades the more powerful nations in particular had decided that little could be accomplished at the U.N. and had turned to individual and private negotiations with other countries, virtually ignoring the forum the U.N. offered.

A third reason for the American attitude toward the U.N. was that the nation had become very isolationist since Vietnam. Many Americans believed that the United States should concentrate on its own problems and let the rest of the world alone. They chose not to believe that the troubles between Israel and the Arab countries in the Middle East could affect them or that their lives could be influenced by whether or not emerging African nations adopted democratic or communist forms of government. Andrew Young's predecessor, Daniel Patrick Moynihan, had voiced the American attitude toward the U.N. during his term as ambassador. So strident had been his criticism of the U.N., and particularly its Third World member nations, that columnist James Reston had called him "the first ambassador against rather than to the United Nations."

Andrew Young hoped to change all that. Unlike his predecessor, he believed in the United Nations. Unlike American isolationists, he believed that the United States was affected by what happened in the rest of the world and that if it did not start showing active interest, particularly in the emerging African nations, it would one day regret it. In his view, the world was no longer a collection of individual independent nations, but was fast becoming a system of "five worlds": the industrial nations; the oil-rich and mineral-rich emerging nations; the developing countries such as the People's Republic of China, Kenya, and India; the nations he called the "poorest of the poor"; and the multinational corporations. In that system the United States would no longer be the dominant power, and in order to survive in that new system would have to deal successfully with all "five worlds." To do that, Young believed, the United States would have to be on the right side of moral issues, and he believed that the greatest moral issue was racism.

Andrew Young intended to address the issue of racism. He accepted the U.N. ambassadorship on the condition that he would have a voice in U.S. foreign policy and that he would be free to speak his mind, even if he disagreed with the President. He realized that he would be unable to change either the image of the U.N. or U.S. policy single-handedly, but he was determined to make an impact.

Having presented his credentials to Secretary-General Waldheim, Young went to the headquarters of the United States mission to the United Nations to greet his staff, who awaited him eagerly. The number of well-wishers and their attitude was astonishing to veteran observers at the U.N. As one reported, ". . . hundreds of staff members turned out for the event, some climbing on chairs for a glimpse—this from a crowd that scarcely bothers to crane for royalty or the appearance of a visiting prime minister." Not just the staff of the U.S. mission was excited about Andrew Young's arrival. Everyone at the U.N., not to mention people in diplomatic circles around the world, was excited about his coming. Partly, of course, this was because he was the first black to hold the position, but more importantly it was because he had such close ties to the President.

Young greeted the staff and thanked them for their expressions of support. Then he set right to the work of being an ambassador, his own way. He wanted to follow an informal style, one that involved many meetings with diplomats of other nations at their own missions, and on that first day in his new job he visited the Israeli delegate, a group of African delegates, a member of the Soviet mission, and the acting head of the British mission. He later attended several receptions in his honor, so by the time he returned to his suite in the nearby Waldorf Towers it was late.

The suite was the official residence of the U.S. Ambassador and it was large enough to accommodate a family, but Young would be leading an essentially bachelor existence there until June. Jean and the children would remain in their home in Atlanta until school was over for the year, and considering the schedule Andrew had lined up for the next few months he would see his family only rarely.

Even though it was late at night by the time he got to his suite, his first day in his new job was not over. He still had to go over his notes about things he wanted to discuss with the Latin American, Asian, and Arab diplomats before he left for Africa on his first official trip as U.S. Ambassador.

Talks on transition from white to black rule in Rhodesia had recently broken down when Rhodesian whites had rejected British proposals for transition to black rule, but Young did not think that the breakdown meant the end of the talks. He was hoping that during his trip he could help find a way to get the talks started again. En route to Africa he would stop in London to see the British chairman of the stalled talks, and in Nigeria and Tanzania he would have the opportunity to confer with a number of African chiefs of state who would be attending an anniversary celebration in Tanzania.

Reporters wanted to know whether Young planned to discuss with these chiefs of state the presence of Cuban troops in Angola. They were referring to statements he had made in a television interview program on January 25. There had been a civil war in Angola and the faction that had ultimately triumphed had asked Cuba to send troops to the country to help. The Cuban troops were still there, and the nations of the West were concerned that their presence might foreshadow armed conflict in southern Africa, which included both Rhodesia and South Africa. When asked how he felt about the situation, Andrew Young had said he thought the presence of the Cuban troops had brought "a certain stability and order" to Angola. The remark had caused controversy because it appeared that the U.S. Ambassador-designate supported the presence of troops from a communist country in Africa. He had meant that the Cuban troops were a stabilizing force because they were keeping the airports open, repairing the telephone and plumbing systems, operating the fishing fleets, even protecting the installations of the U.S.-based multinational corporation, Gulf Oil. He had not meant to defend the Cuban intervention and in fact thought it was wrong, but his positive remark about the Cuban troops got all the attention. It was a diplomatic blunder, and he was not even officially the U.S. Ambassador yet.

When reporters asked him about the Cuban troops on the eve of his departure for Africa, Young realized that they would like nothing better than to re-engage him in that controversy. He refused to give them the opportunity, saying that was not one of the topics on his trip's agenda.

Young spent twelve days abroad. He visited several African countries and many African leaders. He also paid a visit to Robert Sobukwe and took him a copy of Alex Haley's novel *Roots*. He often urged Africans to read about slavery in the United States, explaining, "You might find it easier to read because it happened to us. I could never read much about our own system of enslavement—I got too emotional and too involved. I could read about what happened to Jews in Europe, and I could read about the oppression of blacks in South Africa, but I couldn't read about my own situation. So maybe you can read about ours and gain some insights."

On his return from Africa, Young went to Washington to confer with the President and with officials at the State Department. His position at the State Department was emphasized by his having an office on the seventh floor, the same floor where the Secretary of State, Cyrus Vance, had his office, and by the position of his name in the number two spot on the building's directory, under that of Vance. He then returned to New York and the U.N., where the staff of the U.S. mission greeted him uneasily. He had hinted that he would be making some staff changes, and in his first meeting with the mission staff he said he would be bringing to New York the men and women who had been with him in the civil rights movement and on his congressional staff, people like Stoney Cooks. These new people would, he said, bring more diversity to the mission and would fill mission jobs with the type of people—women and ethnic minorities—who had been too long ignored. Although he said that none of the current staff would be dismissed, he was not believed. The staff feared not just for their own jobs but for the effectiveness of the mission if the new ambassador brought in too many outsiders unfamiliar with the workings of diplomacy.

In the end, the staff concluded their fears had been essentially groundless. No one lost his or her job, and the new ambassador's choices to fill the top four positions on his staff were approved, for they were people with previous experience in the Foreign Service. What Young did get rid of were most of the Cadillacs that had been traditionally available to his office, substituting less pretentious and more economical Ford sedans.

There were other ways in which he brought greater informality to the office. It was not unusual for him to go to the mission in jeans on a Saturday, and on occasion he would invite his chauffeur to have lunch with him in his quarters. Because he was away from his family he was lonely at times, but he got a lot of reading done, alone in the Waldorf suite

Young brought a more informal style to the U.S. Ambassador's post. Sometimes he would serve guests himself, instead of relying on servants. Sometimes he would invite his chauffeur to have lunch with him in his suite.

(WIDE WORLD PHOTOS)

late at night. "He is an avid reader," says Jean Young. "He reads just about everything that he can get his hands on—not just books and articles and newspapers to keep up on all the issues, but good novels that give different insights into people."

Just about a month after he took his new position, Andrew Young settled into a period of work at the U.N. and the diplomats there got their first real opportunity to see him in operation. During most of the previous four weeks he had been either abroad or in Washington, D.C. He had made no major U.N. speeches and had presided over no committee meetings. But he was expected to be at the U.N. now for at least a month, for on March 1 he began a month-long term as president of the Security Council, a position that passes on a rotating basis among the member nations. Veteran diplomats had heard that he hoped to bring to the U.N. the political style that he had found so successful in Congress, one that emphasized talks and meetings in informal situations—in the gym or the congressional cloakroom or private offices—rather than speeches and debates on the House floor. They looked forward to seeing how that strategy would work.

"I think that the first time that we ever sat down with the African delegates and discussed with them what we were thinking in advance—and got their opinions on it and worked it out before we went out on the floor—was when I was president of the Security Council," says Young. "Nobody had ever done that before. Either you try to sneak something by or you try to bully them over, but nobody had ever sat down with them and said, 'Look, this is what we're thinking about. What do you think of it?'" The strategy worked well. The African delegates responded to this show of respect for their opinions, as did the other delegations Young approached in this manner.

But some diplomats feared that Young might view the U.N. as similar to Congress in another way, as a place where members could express their personal views freely without worrying that their remarks would be mistaken for government policy. Already he had made remarks that veteran diplomats considered inappropriate.

In the middle of March, their fears seemed to be confirmed. In the course of Security Council discussions on Rhodesia, Andrew Young suggested that American troops could be used as part of a peace-keeping force during that country's transition from white minority to black majority rule. In making this suggestion, he was only saying openly what many American diplomats were saying in private, that "no one has any confidence in the British" to work out a solution in Rhodesia, and that because the U.S. Army had "the only really integrated units" in the world, it "could play a role in peace-keeping" in Rhodesia. But when the U.S. Ambassador to the U.N. made such statements in public, they were bound to be viewed as official U.S. policy, which they were not.

The next day, Young found himself bombarded with questions from reporters. Forced to explain his remarks, he admitted that sending U.S. troops to Rhodesia would be politically impossible. He also insisted that he was not criticizing the British: "What I said was that [former Secretary of State Henry] Kissinger started a process which he could not finish, and that the British were left holding the bag."

In Washington, some congressmen grumbled about Andrew Young's seeming penchant for making controversial remarks. When Democratic Representative Clement Zablocki, chairman of the House International Relations Committee, complained to Vance, the Secretary of State said that Young was not stating U.S. policy. Zablocki replied, "If he is saying this as Ambassador to the U.N., others will perceive it *is* our policy." More than one critic said that Andrew Young ought to be fired.

Down in New Orleans, Young's parents worried about how this controversy would affect their son. "I feel very grateful that God has enabled him to accomplish the things he has done," his mother says, "but sometimes when the press gets on him, I feel very frustrated. I don't want him to be hurt." His father says, "The flack doesn't bother me, because I'm confident he can take care of himself. But it might cause a rift, a defensive rift, between him and the President. There's that old saying, divide and conquer, and sometimes I wonder if that's what some people are trying to do. There are some who have never accepted the relationship between the President and a black man."

The President stood by his black Cabinet member. He did not suggest that Young refrain from making controversial remarks in the future. Indeed, in his first few months in office President Carter had been pretty outspoken himself about foreign affairs. He had sounded a call for human rights that some feared had so alienated the Soviet Union that the Strategic Arms Limitation Talks between the two countries were in danger. He had openly voiced support of the inclusion of the Palestine Liberation Organization in any lasting settlement in the Middle East, which had angered Israel. He would soon suggest the creation of a "homeland" for Palestinian refugees but in such imprecise terms that neither the Arabs nor the Israelis would know what he meant. He believed in speaking out, in honesty no matter how blunt, for he felt that there had been too much secrecy and too little honesty in the foreign relations of previous administrations. So he understood Andrew Young.

For his part, Young considered quieting down a bit. "Whatever I say, someone wants to blame the U.S. Government for it," he complained. But he still firmly believed in speaking his mind, although he realized he was taking a gamble. "If this style of openness in foreign policy works and I can deliver at the U.N., I'll be vindicated," he said. "If it doesn't work, then I tried and didn't quite make it. But I am determined to try."

True to his word, Andrew Young kept on being open—and kept on getting into trouble. Early in April, he was interviewed in New York by the British Broadcasting Corporation for a television program to be aired in England. In the course of the interview it was suggested that the United States had a racism problem, whereupon Andrew smiled and countered that sometimes he thought Britain was "a little chicken" on racial issues at home as well as in Rhodesia and that Britain had "invented racism." British reaction to the remarks was swift and angry. Britain's chief delegate to the U.N., Ivor Richard, had recently presided over a conference on Rhodesia in Geneva and he was offended by Young's statement. He sent a message to that effect to Andrew. The press called it a reprimand, but Richard took issue with that word. "I see a lot of Andy Young and enjoy working with him," he said. "I would not dream of doing anything so magisterial as trying to reprimand him."

Andrew regretted the remarks. Although he believed Britain was and had been racist, he had not intended his remarks to reflect on Richard personally. He liked the man and knew that he was working hard to bring about a successful solution to Rhodesia's problems. He sent a letter of apology to Richard and at a U.N. reception two days after the broadcast he apologized to him personally as well. "It was the worst day of my life," he said.

Richard accepted both apologies. He sympathized with Andrew's problems in adjusting to the peculiar customs of diplomacy, which has been called the art of lying for your country. He recalled that he had had similar problems when he had gone to the U.N. after ten years in the British House of Commons. Both men were eager to end the matter, and

Richard's refusal to engage in recriminations did stop the press from making more of it, but that did not cause reporters to lay off the U.S. Ambassador.

He was, in press terms, "good copy." Because he was so open, he was very quotable. Many reporters liked him personally, but their first allegiance was to their jobs, which had become more interesting than they had been in a long time for those whose beat was the U.N. They were accustomed to straining to make dull reports interesting, to write stories about diplomats whose favorite answer to them was "no comment." Although Daniel Moynihan had made very quotable statements, they had usually been measured, and he had said "no comment" many times. Andrew Young was different. "I hate to look another human being in the eye and say 'No comment,'" he told one reporter, and the press loved him for it. But that did not stop them from trying to make him want to eat his words many times. There is an old saying: All is fair in love and war. Reporters would add a new twist to it: All is fair in love and war and news gathering.

Down in Atlanta, Jean Young could not help being troubled by the press reports about her husband. "I think the first ones, the very first controversies over his statements, created the most pressure for me," she says. "Because I knew exactly what he was saying, and I knew exactly what he meant, and I couldn't understand why people interpreted it otherwise. I couldn't understand why they would headline the papers with these kinds of statements when, at their essence, they were simple truths that everybdy knew existed."

The furor over his statements bothered Andrew, too. "I wake up every morning at five A.M. worried to death, waiting for them to drop the newspaper at the door so I can see what I've

His first few months in office were a strain for Young. Nearly every public statement he made caused controversy.

(UPI)

UNITED STATES

done today," he admitted. But he was not a newcomer to public life and he realized he should not take the press reports too seriously. He often joked with reporters about them. "Because of me you guys have jobs," he'd say. On April 19 he was about to begin an address to the United Nations Association of the United States when his microphone went dead. After a new microphone was provided, he accused his deputy, James Leonard, of carrying out a threat to "pull the plug" if he made any off-the-cuff remarks. The audience laughed. "I will not be silenced," he declared, and the audience broke into applause. Still, Young refrained from making controversial remarks for a while after the BBC broadcast.

Young visited Africa as U.S. Ambassador to the U.N. a second time in May 1977. He had several purposes in making the trip. One was to stimulate a debate on foreign policy in the United States. He had no doubt that the American press would cover the trip thoroughly and he hoped the American public would begin to consider again the possibility that the United States could be a force for justice in the world. He did not regard the trip as likely to accomplish this, but he saw it as one of many actions he and the rest of the Carter Administration would take to bring about this restoration of faith in America.

Another purpose was to assure the moderate African states that the United States was not forsaking them in favor of nonaligned, Marxist-oriented African states. And finally, he wanted to impress on all African states the sincerity of the Carter Administration's commitment to bringing about social and political change in southern Africa, and to this end he hoped to make a visit to South Africa. But when his representatives first contacted the government of South Africa, they were told that he would not be welcome there. Young hoped that Prime Minister John Vorster would change his mind before he had to return to the United States.

First stop was the Ivory Coast and a conference of American diplomats to various African nations. There he was warmly greeted, for despite some confusion on the part of the participants about just who was responsible for voicing U.S. policy toward Africa, they were delighted at the opportunity to have such a conference, the first such conference in seven years, and at the idea that Andrew Young seemed genuinely interested in their opinions. The Republican administrations during those years, they hinted, had not been very much interested. "Maybe it is just an exercise in ego," said one of the participants in the conference, "but diplomats have egos and it's really nice to stand up and say what you think and have the impression that someone is listening."

Andrew Young did quite a lot of listening during that trip, which did after all include a visit to South Africa. Vice-President Walter Mondale was meeting in Vienna, Austria, with John Vorster, the Prime Minister of South Africa, and Young flew to that city to talk with the two men. There, Vorster changed his mind and said he would not object to Young's visiting his country. The next day Young arrived in Johannesburg, South Africa's largest city.

Security was elaborate. Among other problems, the country was divided over the question of the U.S. Ambassador. Most whites were upset over his agreement with a suggestion that the South African government was "illegitimate" and over his frequent comparisons between the civil rights movement in the United States and the situation in southern Africa. South African blacks, on the other hand, supported him and applauded his statements. There were no serious incidents, and when Andrew spoke to a group of South African businessmen and political leaders he read from a prepared speech. In it, he did not stress the moral questions to which the racial situation in South Africa gave rise. Instead he stressed the economic ones, appealing to their self-interest.

"I inevitably draw upon my experiences in the South and you can do with them what you will," he said. "I'm not trying to give advice to anybody from here, black or white. I'm merely saying this is a possibility amongst many possibilities. And you decide, but don't ever give up. Don't ever say that there is no possibility, don't ever say that there is nothing for which we can hope; don't ever say that we must prepare to fight to the death. Look instead to paths through which you might live and prosper in happiness together.

"But there's a funny thing about capitalism, and I almost hate to call it that. Because it's not what the sociologists write about, or what they used to write about as capitalism in the nineteenth century. Something happens to capitalism when the poor rise up. The system that we enjoy in the United States is a system born of struggle. Yes, it's also a system which was built on the inhumanity of human slavery. But somehow those very slaves who at one point in our history created the cheap labor force which enabled that system to take off and thereby made industrialization possible—those same slaves and their children's children came back again in the fifties and sixties and humanized that system."

Young spoke about how the major impact of the civil rights movement in the U.S. South had been economic, how black boycotts of goods in white-owned stores had helped to bring about an end to segregation, how the Birmingham, Alabama, victory had come about largely because the two largest employers in Birmingham had finally realized segregation was bad for their image, how increased black employment in the United States South as a result of the civil rights struggle had benefited the economy of the South.

"I want to say one word of a rather moral nature," he continued, "and I didn't want to moralize, but I am a preacher, so forgive me. I'm trying to talk about economic realities, but one of the things we all have to face in spite of our level of prosperity and education and culture, is that there is a sense in which it's an accident of birth. That but for the grace of God any of us might have been born poor [and black]—and we have no choice in that. And my opportunity to be born in a relatively secure family in the United States always accompanied with it admonitions from my grandmother which I share with you from the Bible, 'To them to whom much is given, of them will much be required.' "

Young did not visit Soweto, the suburb of Johannesburg where over a million blacks live and which had been the scene of riots a few months earlier. He didn't want to risk causing friction with the government. But he did meet secretly with a group of teen-age students from Soweto who slipped onto a mining magnate's estate to see him. (After Young left, South African officials set out to try to find and question the students.) He did not exhort black South Africans to rise up; yet he did admit, "It would be quite hypocritical if the United States, which had to take up arms to get its freedom from the British, were to go around advising people against it." He did not go around preaching morality, but he did make that mention of the Bible and God in his speech to the South African businessmen. He did not advise black South Africans to engage in economic boycotts, but he did mention that such boycotts and other economic campaigns had worked well in the civil rights movement in the United States. In all, he was quite diplomatic while still managing to get his point across. Thirty-one hours after he had arrived in South Africa he left the country unharmed and without having had to apologize for any of the statements he had made.

Andrew left South Africa having pleased none of its factions, except the moderate blacks. Government officials charged that by talking about economic boycotts, he had broken a pledge not to say anything inflammatory. Militant blacks felt he was being naïve in suggesting that real change could come about in southern Africa by nonviolent means, and were angry about his refusal to denounce the white governments of South Africa and Rhodesia. Only moderate blacks were pleased by the way he had conducted himself on his visit. Still, although the government had no intention of backing down from its plan to create nine independent "homelands" for blacks, perhaps partly in response to Andrew Young's visit it took steps to hasten its plan to ease petty racial restrictions, such as banning blacks from owning homes outside the homelands. Young considered that a victory in itself.

Unfortunately, press coverage of his trip did not end in South Africa. Talking with reporters as the U.S. Air Force plane crossed Africa on its way to London, Young, thinking he was talking "off the record," called the Russians "the worst racists in the world," said the Swedes were "terrible racists" who treated blacks as badly as they were treated in the New York City borough of Queens, and said Britain's "old colonial mentality" was still "very strong throughout the island." Arriving in London, he spoke with reporters there and remarked that the presence of Cuban military advisers in Ethiopia "might not be a bad thing" if they could halt the killings in that country.

When his plane landed in Washington, D.C., Andrew Young found himself in an all too familiar situation—at the center of controversy. Although neither the Russians, the Swedes nor the British liked his statements alleging their racism, the strongest reactions of all came from Queens politicians. They charged that Young knew nothing about the borough and were surprised to hear that of all the places he had called racist he knew more from personal experience about Queens than about any of the others. He had lived in Queens for four years.

Jimmy Breslin, a reporter for a New York newspaper and a resident of Queens, decided to find out whether there was any truth to Andrew Young's remarks. He reported talking to a white resident of Queens who informed him that Hollis, Queens, where the Youngs had lived, was now so full of blacks that "*nobody* lives there anymore." Blacks in Queens sought out reporters to remind them that white residents of Forest Hills, Queens, had demonstrated for a year against the building of a public housing development that was intended to provide housing outside slum areas for low-income tenants. "Andy Young is telling the truth," they said.

Rarely were similar attempts made to investigate the truth or falsity of Young's remarks. When such attempts were made, his statements were usually found to be justified. "If you look at the controversial statements that I've made," he says, "it's very hard to find anywhere in the press where anybody either in the government or in the press has refuted those statements —has said they are wrong. What they've said is that diplomats shouldn't talk that way, he's too controversial, he's not effective. I don't care about being controversial. The prime issue is doing what's right for this country. My telling it like it is has given this country more credibility than we've had since before the war in Vietnam. And if diplomacy is the art of lying for your country, then I'm never going to be a diplomat."

As usual, what was missing in the furor was any sense of the context in which his "headline" remarks had been made. Only one publication, *Newsweek*, mentioned that he had made the remarks in the course of a discussion on racism. Talking about what he felt might have been accomplished by his visit to South Africa, he had said he had the feeling that things might get worse instead of better but at least he hoped his visit would encourage the South Africans to talk more about racism. As the *Newsweek* reporters explained, ". . . the point of his homebound soliloquy on racism was that prejudice is declining only in places where the subject is constantly discussed."

Young's remarks about Cuban advisers in Ethiopia were another matter, because they seemed to contradict U.S. policy.

The very day he had made his remarks in London, the U.S. Department of State in Washington had expressed concern about the presence of those advisers and had said it would be a serious development if the rumors proved true that four to five hundred Cuban soldiers would be sent to Ethiopia soon. Andrew Young knew this. He mentioned those statements and guessed he should express grave doubts, too, but when a reporter asked whether it came from the heart, he said, "No, it really does not, because [the Ethiopians] are killing people right and left, and I guess I think that maybe the Cubans may be a little more rational than the Ethiopians at this point."

Young had not talked about Cuban fighting troops, only about Cuban advisers, so the contradiction was not as serious as the press tried to make it. Still, the ambassador had openly disagreed with the State Department once again, and it was the stuff of headlines.

Andrew Young kept on talking, especially about racism. In an interview published in the July issue of *Playboy* magazine and available on the stands in mid-June, he described both former Presidents Gerald Ford and Richard Nixon as "racists" and provoked yet another controversy. William E. Brock, chairman of the Republican National Convention, said his remark "points up the fact that he is a diplomatic incompetent who should be fired." Brock added, "The very least that President Carter can do is demand an apology from Young."

Brock's statement and those of other critics bothered Young. He had used the word "racism" and did not regret it because he thought it was appropriate. "Unfortunately, I haven't been able to find a word other than racism. I wish I could, because people react emotionally to that word and don't pay attention to what I'm trying to say," he explained. But he did worry that people were beginning to blame the President for things he said. Because he planned to be in Washington the next day for a committee hearing, he asked for an appointment with

President Carter and planned to ask to be treated from then on not as a friend but as an ambassador, subject to correction and criticism from the President.

The hearing was being held by the House International Relations Committee, whose chairman, Clement Zablocki, had been very critical of Andrew Young in the past. Much of its business was devoted to Young's *Playboy* interview, and he was asked whether his definition of racism would not apply to Presidents Kennedy and Johnson as well as to their two Republican successors. He said that it would. Chairman Zablocki asked if Young would now try harder to be "more of an ambassador and less of a politician," and Young said he couldn't promise. He said he would "much rather be fired for trying to do what is right to help the country, than to be a retired successful ambassador who never did anything." The committee did not censure him. Given time to explain his views, he never came out sounding strident. Questioners on television news interview programs learned this, too. "Why haven't you made any controversial statements during this program?" they would ask. And Young would answer, "Because I have had half an hour to talk."

President Carter read the *Playboy* interview and understood Andrew Young's remarks in the context of his theory that an insensitivity to differences in race and culture equals racism and that such insensitivity handicaps American foreign policy in countries with non-white majorities. The President thought Young's language might have been a bit strong, but, as Young later told reporters, "he didn't tell me to shut up." In fact, Carter later told his Cabinet members in a meeting that Andrew Young would go down in history as a great man and instructed his press office to relay the remark to reporters.

Responding to Carter's reaction, some observers declared that the President was supporting Andrew Young because he did not want to admit he had chosen the wrong man as Ambassador to the U.N. But others believed the President's response was not that political or self-serving. Carter supported Young, they said, because he agreed with his policy of public frankness and disagreed with the traditional way of doing things at the State Department and other bastions of U.S. diplomacy.

Early in his presidency, Carter had made some remarks about "defensible borders" for Israel that had caused consternation in the State Department. The Department had issued a "clarification" of the President's remarks. At his first town meeting in Clinton, Massachusetts, in March, Carter had endorsed the idea of a "homeland for the Palestinians." No American President or diplomat had ever uttered that phrase officially. After the meeting, the President had called the State Department to tell them what he had said and asked that no clarification be issued.

A lot of Andrew Young's supporters and friends breathed a sigh of relief when they heard how the meeting had gone. They were really getting worried that Young would not be able to get out of trouble, and they were worried that he had changed. But they learned the same thing that interviewers on half-hour television programs had learned, that if Andrew Young's whole conversations were reported they would not be all that controversial.

An old friend explained, "I have never known Andy to be strident. All these things seemed too out of character." The friend, who was a congressman, had not seen much of Young since he had become an ambassador, but he could not believe his friend had changed that much in such a short time. So, he attended the House International Relations Committee hearing and came away both impressed and relieved: "He did a superb job explaining some complicated thoughts and positions. And when you give him an hour or two to talk about his views, there is no stridency. It's the same Andy Young I've known—cool, articulate, and reasonable. But when you try to encapsulate what he was saying in a thirty-second television news spot or a headline, I can see why it comes out strident."

Man with a Mission / 169

So often the problem was one of context. In the *Playboy* interview, Young had said that Nixon and Ford "were racists . . . not in the aggressive sense but in that they had no understanding of the problems of colored peoples anywhere. There's a sense in which every American, black or white, is affected by racism. You cannot grow up in the United States of America in the twentieth century and not be tainted by it."

The headlines had been very succinct: "Nixon and Ford Racists, says Young." A reader is bound to react differently to that kind of headline from the way he reacts to the paragraph in which that kind of statement is made.

Many members of the House Committee on International Relations agreed with Andrew Young's statement, and most praised him for speaking out honestly and raising the issue of race. Republican John Buchanan of Alabama told the committee that southerners best understood Andrew Young's belief that racism is found far beyond the South and that it affects most people. President Carter was a southerner and perhaps that is one reason he understood Andrew Young so well. But even non-southerners like Secretary of State Cyrus Vance and most of his colleagues in the United Nations supported him.

Young's major problem was that he had become such a media figure, such a newsworthy personality. He was the most visible U.S. Ambassador to the United Nations to come along in years, if not in the history of the U.N. He had used his celebrity to get the American people thinking more about international relations and particularly about Africa. He had also used his notoriety to get people in the United States thinking more about the effects of racism at home and abroad. But he had also established himself as a media figure who almost guaranteed controversial news copy. When he went to Pennsylvania to make a speech he was asked in all seriousness by a local reporter, "Do you plan to say anything outrageous while you're here?"

11 / Andrew Young Today ...
and Tomorrow

The rest of the Young family arrived in New York in June.
They had never lived in an apartment before. When Young
was a congressman, he had maintained an apartment in Washington, D.C., for a while, but "home" had always been a house.
Between January, when Young moved into the Waldorf Towers
suite, and June, when the family arrived, he and Jean had
talked about how the move would affect the family. Says Jean
Young, "It was a question of, how do we move into this kind
of luxurious, prestigious residence, where former ambassadors
have lived, with a fourteen-year-old dog, a five-year-old child,
and a teen-ager?"

Feeling they might all be better off in a house, even if it was
in the middle of New York City, Andrew had looked around
for one. He found the search frustrating. The U.N. Ambassa-

dor's official residence couldn't be just any old house: it had to be a nice house and close to the U.N. When word got out that he was looking at a $600,000 Fifth Avenue mansion, some reporters suggested that he didn't think the Waldorf was "good enough" for him. That was not the point at all. "The Waldorf is very nice, and it's convenient, but I just have problems trying to bring up a small child in a hotel," Young explained. He and Jean decided that it would be best to avoid more controversy, so they decided to make the best of the situation. Late in June, Jean Young, Paula and Bo, and the dog, Snuffy, arrived with clothing and toys, records and dog biscuits, to take up residence at the Waldorf Towers.

"It required some adjustments on everyone's part," laughs Jean Young, referring to the fact that none of the previous ambassadors had had small children. "But I have to admit the staff has been marvelous. The elevator operators and maids and everyone else have sort of adopted the whole family."

The dog was the only casualty. "We eventually had to send Snuffy back to my mother in Alabama," she says. "The steps got a little too much for her." But the Young family numbered four only a short time. The oldest daughter, Andrea, decided to attend Columbia Law School, so she came to live at the Waldorf, and a third Sobukwe, nineteen-year-old Dalendgabo, joined the family. What with visits from daughter Lisa, the two older Sobukwe children, Jean's family and Andrew's family, not to mention all their friends, the U.S. Ambassador's official suite is a very active place.

As the wife of the U.S. Ambassador, Jean Young is required to do a great deal of entertaining. On the average, she presides over three or four luncheons and dinners every week. Although she was used to entertaining and had given many large parties without professional help, she found that it was very nice to have the Waldorf staff pitch in. And there are, of course, other advantages to living at the Waldorf. But Jean Young is as unpretentious as her husband, and one of the first things she did was to bring more informality to the official luncheons and dinners and receptions she and Andrew hosted. She began inviting family and friends to them, which not only provided a more personal air to the gatherings but also gave foreign guests a chance to meet other Americans. Andrew's parents attended a dinner for members of the Russian delegation. The Young children attended a reception for African representatives, who were encouraged to bring their children, too.

Mrs. Young also varied the standard banquet fare at times. "At an official dinner for the Chinese delegation, we served soul food," she laughs, "and they loved it! I had to import the collard greens from Atlanta, to ensure their authenticity. It was a great evening."

Someday, Ambassador and Mrs. Young want to have an "All-American" party for some of the foreign representatives. They will ask all their guests to wear casual clothes like blue jeans, and they will serve hot dogs and hamburgers and potato salad. "I know when we go to foreign countries we do not like 'American' events set up for us," Jean Young says. "We prefer things that are indigenous to the country—things that show us what the people of that country normally do to enjoy themselves."

Although he was happy to have his family with him again, Andrew Young realized that in New York they would be more exposed than ever to the extensive media coverage of him. So he tried to tone down his media image and to be careful that his statements were not taken out of context. He started carrying a small tape recorder, which he turned on whenever he talked with reporters, and by August he was giving more attention to Third World countries other than Africa.

President Carter had suggested that Young "shift his emphasis more toward other developing nations outside Africa," and he was an obvious choice to head a mission to the Caribbean where he was applauded for his outspokenness on African

Andrew Young likes to involve his children in his activities as often as possible. Here, five-year-old Bo accompanies him to the Security Council and meets Israel's Ambassador, Chaim Herzog.

nationalism and on racism. On August 5 he and Mrs. Young, in the company of half a dozen economic and political advisers, embarked on a twelve-day, ten-country trip in the Caribbean to improve U.S. relations with those countries and to get information to help in the development of an over-all Caribbean policy for the Carter Administration to pursue.

The Administration was concerned that the Caribbean was leaning too heavily toward communism. The influence of President Fidel Castro of Cuba was growing, and Jamaica and Guyana had endorsed the Cuban intervention in Angola on behalf of the Marxist Popular Movement, which had triumphed in the civil war. The Carter Administration also hoped Andrew's tour would emphasize the positive side of its concern for human rights. Whereas it had until then pointed up abuses, here it could applaud respect for human rights on the part of many of the Caribbean countries. Most of these countries had a good record of preserving constitutional government and protecting civil liberties. Support for them economically would be a way of showing recognition of their favorable human rights records.

And finally, the President hoped the trip would take some of the public attention off Andrew Young and his African diplomacy. As one of the staff of the State Department explained, "Carter had to do it. He had to take some of the pressure off Andy for a while—the press was killing him."

The move did not come in time to take the pressure off Andrew Young in the eyes of some congressmen. At the end of July the Conservative Caucus and its "Citizen's Cabinet," a self-proclaimed shadow government, started a campaign to oust him from his position through a mailing that solicited support and contributions. The letter was signed by Meldrim Thomson, Jr., the Governor of New Hampshire at that time. Andrew Young, who just a year earlier had been said to have "no real enemies," had some powerful ones now.

The Caribbean trip was a pleasant one. In Jamaica, the first

*On his forty-sixth birthday, Young waits with his daughter Andrea
to appear on a segment of television's "Meet the Press."*

stop, Andrew recalled how twenty years earlier he had been so impressed with the country that he had saved up to bring his mother, father, wife, and children to visit so they too could see a place where blacks did well. After stopping next in Mexico, he went on to Costa Rica where he received a warm welcome from the Costa Rican Foreign Minister, Dr. Gonzalo Facio. Facio had spent years as ambassador in Washington, D.C., and had heard Dr. Martin Luther King's "I have a dream" speech on the steps of the Lincoln Memorial in 1963. He was eager to meet the man who had been so close to King. So was the President of Costa Rica, Daniel Oduber, who had suggested to Rosalynn Carter during her trip to Latin America that the President send Andrew Young on this tour because his reformist approach would be refreshing. Costa Rica had begun a campaign for a human rights commissioner in the United Nations, but thus far it had been blocked by the Soviet Union and others who objected to it as an infringement of their sovereignty. Costa Rican officials hoped Young's tour might encourage other Latin American countries to support the campaign.

On to Guyana, where Young met with black Rhodesian nationalist leader Joshua Nkomo, who was touring black Caribbean countries, seeking support, and found Nkomo more willing to talk about compromise in the Rhodesian situation than he had been before. With Guyanese officials, Young discussed U.S. aid and greater cooperation between the two countries. The mere fact that they were engaging in discussions, both sides emphasized, was a positive step. Guyana leans toward socialism and was not given much attention by the earlier, Republican administrations. Something the Guyana foreign minister, Fred Wills, said caused Young to smile and he encouraged Wills to repeat it to reporters so they could in turn help put Americans' minds at ease about the United States dealing with a socialist country. Wills told Andrew that the

Jean Young accompanies her husband abroad whenever she can, but both are usually too busy to do much sightseeing.

(WIDE WORLD PHOTOS)

Guyanese were more interested in the American entertainers Stevie Wonder and Diana Ross than they were in the Soviet musicians Prokofiev and Shostakovich.

The next stop was Trinidad, then Venezuela, and then Haiti. There had been some criticism of the visit to Haiti, a country with one of the worst human rights records in the Western Hemisphere. The critics had charged that Young's visit to Haiti would be like a sanction of its policies, but Young insisted that his primary reason for visiting the country was to remind its President-for-life, Jean-Claude Duvalier, of the Carter Administration's human rights policy. He had intended to do so privately, but he did not like the hostile attitude of Haitian officials, so while in Haiti he delivered a surprisingly blunt public message on human rights in which he warned Haitian officials, although not in so many words, that American aid might be reduced if something wasn't done to improve the country's human rights record. As he put it, Congress had "ordered us only to spend American tax money where it contributes to human freedom and development." He felt he had accomplished something, for Duvalier promised him he would release at least some political prisoners and implement some reform measures.

All in all, the trip was a successful one. Andrew Young and his advisers had gathered much data on which to base their recommendations to Congress on trade with and U.S. aid to the countries visited. Young had started the trip with some misgivings and had been especially nervous about his visit to Haiti, but he had managed to convince many Latin American leaders that the Carter Administration was genuinely interested in a regional partnership, in helping these countries without meddling unduly in their affairs. What he and Jean, who had been visiting hospitals and museums and meeting with a variety of groups and organizations, regretted was that they had had so little time to enjoy the natural beauties of the countries they had visited. As Young commented ruefully, "One of the ultimate tragedies of this trip is that I've been in some of the most beautiful waters in the world and I've yet to see a beach."

Hardly had they returned to New York when Andrew Young was off again, this time to Zambia to join British Foreign Secretary David Owen in a meeting with five black African presidents and two Rhodesian nationalist leaders to discuss a British-American proposal for ending white minority rule in Rhodesia. When he returned from this trip, he would be in New York to stay awhile, for a new session of the United Nations General Assembly would open in mid-September.

Young returned to New York to discover he was suddenly being given slightly different press coverage from that which he was used to getting. While he was in Zambia, the New York *Times* had carried a very favorable editorial. For a while it had

Andrew Young and British Foreign Minister David Owen vote for the peace proposal they drafted on the Rhodesian situation.

(UPI)

been fashionable to "pick on" Andrew Young, the editorial
read, but now fewer complaints were heard. Indeed, according
to other diplomats, he had become the most effective person in
the United Nations and perhaps the most influential person in
African affairs. He complemented the officials of the State Department, like Secretary of State Cyrus Vance; while they concentrated on the Soviet Union and China and the Middle East,
he concentrated on working out a new relationship between
the United States and the poor and emerging Third World nations. He might talk "undiplomatically" but he did not talk
"idly," and in fact his controversial remarks about racism and
paranoia over communism contained "much good sense."

When Young read the editorial, he was speechless. He'd
become—or tried to become—so accustomed to criticism that he
found it hard to handle praise!

Not many other newspapers or news commentators came out
in support of Andrew Young as had the *Times*. Many still considered him undiplomatic and unable to handle the job. Some
would never admit he could do anything right, because he was
black. Others would never admit he could do anything right,
because he was a liberal. But the constant reportage of his remarks out of context, the constant headlines, and the constant
editorial criticism declined. This decline was not due to any
real change in Andrew Young; he kept on telling the truth as
he saw it, and in language just as controversial as ever. Instead,
the decline was due to a practical realization on the part of
news reporters. As Joseph Lelyveld, a reporter who had followed Young closely since his appointment to the U.N. post,
put it, "The truth is that the story of Young's off-the-cuff remarks died from tedium, once it became clear that he would
not talk himself out of a job."

Three months later, Andrew alluded to the seeming precari-
ousness of his position in the early days of his ambassadorship.

It was his first anniversary as United States Permanent Representative to the United Nations, and he acknowledged that this anniversary had to be one of the major milestones of his career. "A lot of people figured I wouldn't last six months, so I guess I'm ahead of the game," he said.

Although press coverage of his activities had declined somewhat since he was no longer such controversial copy, it was still significant. The activities of Ambassador Andrew Young continued to be reported more extensively than those of previous ambassadors, but that was not just because he was the first black ambassador or the most controversial ever; it was also because he worked very hard at his job, traveled extensively, and addressed a wide range of issues. In November 1977, for example, he proposed a solution to the failure of many developing countries to grow enough food for their people. Addressing a meeting of the United Nations Food and Agriculture Organization in Rome, he suggested that a "food corps" be organized, under which expert volunteers, drawn mostly from the Third World, would go to other Third World countries to teach them how to produce what they needed. His proposal, being noncontroversial, was not widely reported in the press. Yet it was an excellent idea, and one he would work to implement.

His off-the-cuff remarks would still make headlines from time to time. In July 1978, commenting on the trials in the Soviet Union of two dissidents, trials that were causing an uproar in the West, he told a Paris newspaper reporter that "there are hundreds, perhaps thousands, of political prisoners in the United States." He made the statement while trying to explain why he thought the situation of the Soviet dissidents should not be overdramatized, why he thought that, "You cannot stop the world because of a trial no matter where it is and who it is." But his remarks created a furor in the United States, and for the first time people in government challenged him to prove

the truth of his charge. In the Senate, Republican Barry Gold-
water demanded that President Carter dismiss Andrew Young
if he could not supply evidence to support his statement about
American political prisoners. Republican representative of Indiana Dan Quayle made a similar demand in a letter to Carter,
and both Republican national chairman Bill Brock and Georgia
representative Larry McDonald called for Andrew Young's dis-
missal.

Young could not supply the kind of evidence his critics demanded, for his definition of political prisoners was different
from theirs. He did not mean that Americans were in jail because they had written tracts against the government or disagreed publicly with the government. He meant that there
were Americans in jail who would not be there if they were not
poor, or if they were not non-white. As Richard Cohen wrote
in an editorial in the Washington *Post*, "We have always sent
people to jail for essentially political acts or for political reasons. Do you think Martin Luther King was in the Birmingham
jail for being a scofflaw?" Because Andrew Young believes that
almost every facet of society operates on a kind of political
basis, he had used the term "political" to refer to power—who
has it and who doesn't, and what those who have it do to those
who don't.

In making his remarks about "political prisoners" in the
United States, Andrew Young was also expressing his own particular world view. Although he loves the United States, he
does not think that our system is so much better than any
others that he can go around claiming its superiority. And he
does not think the nations of the world can get along very well
if any one of them sets itself above all the others morally, especially when it is not morally perfect itself.

President Carter had made an issue of the trials of the Soviet
dissidents, for he had sounded a call for human rights at the
very beginning of his administration and believed that the

trials were an example of the total denial of human rights. He was displeased with Young's remarks and he told him so. In fact, it was perhaps the greatest test of what has been called the "peculiar alliance" of these two southern men, one black and one white. But the alliance survived.

Over in the House of Representatives, there was a renewed attempt to introduce an impeachment resolution against Andrew Young, an attempt led by his fellow Georgian, Republican Larry McDonald. It was tabled by a vote of 293–82 and thus was essentially voted down. Though he now had important enemies, they were not powerful enough to impeach him.

Not everyone criticized his "political prisoners" statements. Some, like *Washington Post* editorial writer Richard Cohen, wound up supporting him. "Every time you take one of his controversial statements and start to write about it, it begins to make sense," wrote Cohen in a November 1978 editorial. "In the end, all you can do is throw up your hands and say he's right." Elsewhere in the world, Andrew Young had many new friends and supporters, and, weighing the reaction of his statements, positive and negative, he decided that basically he had done the right thing.

"I hate to blame everything I do on God," he says, but in fact his approach to his job at the United Nations was based on a philosophy of which he thinks God would approve. He approached foreign relations much as he had the issues he had dealt with as a congressman, as "people problems." He saw major issues and crises from the viewpoint of the individual. When he was in Congress, he voted on legislation and introduced bills according to how they would affect individual Americans, especially poor, non-white ones. As U.S. Ambassador to the U.N., he found time to be concerned about food production, for he was able to put himself in the position of the poor African who didn't have enough to eat. Even his remarks about American political prisoners came from that kind of thinking. Instead of seeing the United States and the Soviet Union only as nations, he could extend the relationship to that of people who were trying to compromise in order to live in peace together.

Young's "people approach" had worked well, on the whole. He had restored much of the rest of the world's faith in the United States. Representatives of other countries trusted him to speak the truth, for he had certainly gotten himself into a lot of trouble at home by doing so, but hadn't stopped. They also found that Americans had become much better informed about African and other Third World nations, and felt that was a direct result of all the attention paid to Andrew Young. Americans may have read the stories about his controversial remarks to find out what those remarks were, but in the process they had learned a lot about the Third World.

At the beginning of his term, Andrew Young had been considered to be almost obsessed with Africa, a man who wanted singlehandedly to launch a crusade for independence and development there. By the end of his first year in office, his views about African independence and U.S. relations with African countries had become United States policy. What's more, between them Jimmy Carter and Andrew Young had quite effectively moved the United States out of its isolationist doldrums and into a new activism in foreign policy.

There had been bloody strife in Rhodesia. Black terrorists had committed violent crimes against whites. The white government had finally bowed to the inevitability of interracial government and was willing to compromise. The white government of South Africa had refused to learn from the Rhodesian experience and remained firm in its resolve not to share power with its majority black population. All over Africa there were factional disputes and racial disputes and tribal disputes and too much hunger. But there had been progress, and just as when he was in Congress, Andrew Young could see progress in

Young addresses the Americans for Democratic Action prior to his trip to Africa in May 1977. At the time, he was still not sure whether he would be allowed to visit South Africa.

(WIDE WORLD PHOTOS)

little victories. Despite all the pressures, he believed he had been able to make a difference.

Jean Young agrees. She is no longer teaching, but she has much to do as the wife of the U.S. Ambassador to the U.N. Aside from serving on the board of trustees of Manchester College, her alma mater, and of Atlanta Junior College, which she helped to found, she is a member of several committees connected with the U.N. and chairperson of the United States Committee on the International Year of the Child. "I'm enjoying this stage," she says. "The experiences are so broad. Every day you encounter people from every part of the globe, and you come to the realization that *everybody, everywhere* is just 'ordinary folk.' The people you look up to, that you think are running the world, are no different from anyone else when you come in contact with them on an everyday basis. You realize that the poor person down in south Georgia has the same sensitivity and intelligence as some of the people who are heads of state and that it is just experience and exposure that catapults one into one direction and another one into another."

Although Andrew Young travels frequently and rarely ends his day before ten p.m., he is able to be with his family more often now than during either the civil rights or the congressional years. He and Mrs. Young attend receptions at other missions, and host receptions themselves. "The two of us play tennis together frequently," says Jean Young, "and he jogs as often as he can. He loves to jog. He and Bo go to Central Park and Bo rides his bicycle and Andrew jogs along with him. He enjoys being with friends and family, and our relatives visit us as often as they can."

Thus, the United Nations stage of Andrew Young's career and his family's life with him is proving to be quite pleasant in many ways, even though it is not a settled one. Positions like his change with the President and the administration, and so his job will inevitably be affected by the outcome of future presidential elections. What will he do when he leaves the post of United States Permanent Representative to the United Nations? He and Jean really do not know, and are not worried about it.

"I think the thing that has helped us to be as comfortable and as happy in what we are doing as we are is that we have never projected too far into the future," Jean Young says. "We've taken each move, each job, with a certain intensity and dedication—we've put everything into whatever we're done, wherever we've been—and so we'll just take whatever the next step will be and adjust accordingly. So I don't really project long-range. Andrew doesn't either.

"He realizes that there are all kinds of alternatives open to him. He would love to go somewhere and be able to just relax and write. Anyway," she laughs, "that's what he *thinks* he'd like to do. He'd love to just be a lecturer. He'd love to get back into politics at some point perhaps. He'd love to be a minister in a church somewhere.

"So, he feels that no matter where he goes, things will evolve for him and he will be involved. He doesn't feel he has to structure his future. He just has to say, 'Wherever I am, I've got to do whatever it is I feel needs to be done at that moment, and I have to do it well, and with commitment, and with dedication. I can't worry about whether my future is endangered because of what I'm doing; I have to do simply what I think is best at that moment.'

"That's based primarily on his faith," she concludes. "I have no quarrel with that."

Whatever he does, Andrew Young will continue to be interested and involved in the affairs of other countries and in the relationships of those other countries with his own country. And whatever he does, he will bring to it the energy and commitment and indomitable optimism that he has had ever since he first decided to dedicate his life to God. Andrew Young is a man with a mission, and no amount of trouble or pressure will dampen the sense of mission he has. "I believe in this world, even love this world," he says. "I am very aware of its shortcomings, but I can see progress."

In his own way and with total dedication, Andrew Young is working to contribute to that progress.

Index